WELLFLEET *and the* World

Themes of a Cherished and Threatened Place

BRENT HAROLD

KINNACUM PRESS
Wellfleet Massachusetts

Library of Congress Control Number: 2003090772

ISBN 0-9655598-1-5

Cover design by Paula Chance and Brent Harold

KINNACUM PRESS
P.O. Box 1683
Wellfleet MA 02667
e-mail: Kinnacum@capecod.net

Dec. 2004

for my mother, Charlotte Webber Harold

Dear Aunt Gwennie &
Uncle Billy,
Thanks for sharing
your world with us.
Love —
Julia G. Bibby

CONTENTS

Foreword by Ray Oldenburg   ix

Numerical Perspective   xii

Introduction: Confessions of a Washashore   1

94

Essential Regional Terminology   15

At Home With Entropy   18

The Kindness of Strangers   21

The Museumification of Uncle Tim and Aunt Sally   24

Varieties of Human Intervention   27

Coyotes Out of Context   30

95

Rooting for Chaos   35

Nipping Progress in the Bud   38

Two-Thirds Empty Glass   41

Requiem for Shirttail Point   44

Wild East   47

Plastic Donut, Soulful Pizza   50

Dilemma of a Perfect Day at the Ocean   54

Will it Play in Peoria?   57

Stretching the Season   60

96

Development Blues   65

Getting Real   68

Struttin' Our Stuff   71

Pushing the River   74

Wellfleetland   77

The Safe Place Concept   80

97

The Implied Ocean   85

Brave Stand   88

Exorcising the Urban Ghosts   90

What's In a House Name?   93

Submitting to Main Street   97

Mystery fence at Old Pier Road   101

Fairweather Sailor   104

98

Sharing Words   109

Self-Doubt Here in the Middle Period of Mall Proliferation   113

Yee Haw   116

Natural Socialism   119

Vieques' Navy Base, Our National Seashore   122

Fraught with Appreciation   126

The Plugged and the Unplugged   129

A Juice by Any Other Name   132

99

Seeing Our Houses as Others See Them   137

More Solution Than Problem   141

Pounce   144

Jefferson's Kitchen and the C-2 Zone   147

The All-town Town Meeting   150

The Absorbability Theme   153

Obliviousness of Things Past   156

Oasis, Speedbump, Guerilla Base   159

People Chowder   162

The Big and the Small   165

All Game, No Sidelines   168

Being a Hot Commodity   171

To Hang Or Not To Hang   174

Holes In a Town's Soul   177

Go Play in the Street   180

Marginal America   183

00

Sleeping Dog   189

New Cow on the Farm   192

Can't Happen Here   195

Honeymoon Over   198

Lame Ducks   201

Electronic Citizenship   204

Transcending Our Grocery Shopping Dichotomy   207

We Hate When We Do That   210

Our OPM Problem   213

Call of the Wild   216

Outsider Fetish; or, Better the T.A. You Don't Know   219

01

Legislated Diversity in the Latter Days
of the Former Beer Capital of the Western World   223

Truro Golf and the Taliban   226

What Happened in Wellfleet?   229

Original Sin   233

Making An Honest Dump Out of Us   235

Jekyll and Hyde   237

The Little Pharm That Apparently Couldn't   240

Equal Access and the Toilet Analogy   243

Wellfleet and the World: a 9/11Medley   246

Wabi-sabi   253

02

Living with Sand Roads   259

Varieties of Pond Pollution   265

The Aesthetics of Shellfishing   268

The Taboo Logic of Mutual Back-scratching   271

S.T.A.B.L.L.   274

Thanks   277

FOREWORD

When Brent Harold and I first discussed this book, he considered it limited to local interest. I heartily disagreed. Countless towns and urban neighborhoods in the United States are suffering the loss of character and self-determination which endears them to their residents and embeds their families in a supportive social context. Located on picturesque and popular Cape Cod, Wellfleet has much to teach increasingly vulnerable communities throughout the nation.

The author is, in the local vernacular, a "washashore," a late-comer, a person not born in Wellfleet. Though this may not have earned him the bona fides of a true native in the eyes of some, it has afforded him a perspective which the natives do not have. He has lived in those lesser human habitats from which the summer visitors flee. He is familiar with the blandness and sameness and fakery which is coming to town if it is not warded off. His numerous writings in behalf of preserving Wellfleet against the forces which threaten must surely have convinced his readers that a more dedicated and involved citizen would be hard to find anywhere on the Cape.

Of the many threats Brent Harold discusses, none is more insidious than chains and franchises which threaten local control of local affairs, that aspect of American genius that Tocqueville so much admired. The pharmacist, once a person of stature in the community, has been reduced to a "drug-clerk" whom nobody knows. Small towns and urban neighborhoods contained a host of local independent business people who knew everybody in the area and cared about them. Their places were the informal information centers for both locals and visitors. It was often they who informed parents about the aberrant behavior of youth before the police had to. They were also "boosters" of the local community because their fate was tied to it. These citizen-entrepreneurs who play such a vital role in the creation and well-being of the community are increasingly replaced by chain store employees whose job descriptions do not include civic involvement and who are often discouraged from it. Not long after Paul Harvey took money to recite heart-warming anecdotes about Walmart's "caring people," he developed voice problems. I like to think it was divine intervention.

If employees and patrons are reduced by chain store takeover, the town characters, the oddballs, the ones who march to a different drummer are eliminated. These types typically give the community more flavor than trouble, and they have always had to rely upon local businesses far more tolerant and caring than chain stores or mall managers. An architect with digs in London, Vancouver, and San Francisco tells me that, of the three, the last has become his least favorite place. "Now," he says, "It's a town of 700,000 yuppies. The interesting people can't afford to live there."

If anything vies with franchise operations in destroy-ing community and reducing human beings, it is increasingly intrusive government. Federal highway programs have defined scores of cohesive urban neighborhoods as "social debris" and bulldozed them away. Its urban renewal and housing programs have gutted cities, created urban sprawl, and demolished badly needed affordable housing. Separate use zoning, adopted under Hoover, made us excessively automobile dependent and produced a boring habitat wherever single use zoning prevails. Banned from postwar residential areas are all those traditional meeting places in and around which community was once realized.

These are but some of the forces tending to erode Wellfleet's local fabric which columnist Brent Harold has addressed over the years. His book is an education on the concept of a genuine progress, which often means rejecting those "advances" which further alienate us from our fellow human beings as well as adopting those which better our communities. It is also an education in "real community" which Wendell Berry defined as *local*—all else being metaphor. Where we live largely determines how we live and the sterility of the postwar automobile subdivision, as more and more Americans are realizing, is the anti-model. Wellfleet is much closer to what we want. But can it be preserved?

A gentleman on the editorial staff of the *Des Moines Register* recently characterized civic journalism as so much silliness. He couldn't have been more wrong. Consider what San Francisco's Herb Caen, Chicago's Mike Royko and New York's Joseph Mitchell did for their towns. Out on the farther reaches of the Cape Brent Harold continues in the footsteps of Tom Kane, demonstrating that civic journalism is as vital to small towns as it is to large cities. The task is not easy, the victories may be few, but the cause justifies the struggle.

Ray Oldenburg
Pensacola, Florida

NUMERICAL PERSPECTIVE

10,000 BC: Approximate date the glacier deposited the moraine that became Cape Cod.

5000 BC: Approximate date native Americans settled in this area.

2500 BC: Approximate date of great Egyptian pyramids.

1606: First European (Champlain) sails into what was to be Wellfleet Harbor.

1616: Death of Shakespeare.

1620: Pilgrims sail by Great Island, have first encounter with natives in Eastham, then sail on for a hard winter in Plymouth.

1645: Members of Plymouth settlement return to Lower Cape to purchase land now occupied by Orleans, Eastham and Wellfleet, the Eastham grant.

1660: Approximate date of first settlement in Bound Brook area of Billingsgate, as the northern part of the Eastham grant was called then.

1724: Population of Billingsgate approximately 300.

1740: Early environmental concerns lead to legislation to ameliorate effects of deforestation and over-grazing.

1765: Wellfleet's population approximately 928; New York City's population 12,500.

1775: Billingsgate incorporated as Wellfleet; population 1235.

1790: First U.S. census lists 24 "urban places" of population 2500 or more. Wellfleet's approximate population the same year: 1500.

1825: Roughly, the start of today's "central district" laid out along Main Street and Commercial Street. (For the first 150 years or so town consisted of scattered neighborhoods.)

1850: Population 2411, the highest until mid 1980s.

1850s: Thoreau makes a series of visits to Outer Cape using stagecoach and shank's mare.

1859: 12 neighborhood schools scattered throughout town.

1870: Railroad reaches Wellfleet.

1902: Number of town schools reduced to four plus a high school.

1914: Cape Cod Canal opens; roads cross it on drawbridges.

1915: Billingsgate lighthouse automated; last fulltime residents leave.

1935: Present bridges over the Canal open.

1938: Wellfleet Consolidated School built, centralizing all town schools.

1939: Railroad passenger service to Wellfleet ends.

1947. Police department established, consisting of one member, the chief (before that time the chairman of the board of selectman was ex-officio peace officer). Ratio of officers to population: 1 to 1000.

1948: Route 6 bypasses Wellfleet's downtown.

1950: five grocery stores in town, one for each 200 people.

1956: Wellfleet's downtown movie theater (located on site of present Congregational Church parking lot) closes down.

1957: First building regulations establishing setbacks, frontage, minimum lot size (10,000 sq.ft.).

1959: Town votes to join Nauset Regional School District along with Brewster, Orleans and Eastham. Wellfleet Consolidated School becomes Wellfleet Elementary.

Legislation introduced to create Cape Cod National Seashore, including over 60% of Wellfleet land. Much opposition expressed in local hearings.

Mid-Cape Highway completed to Orleans-Eastham Rotary; traditional Route 6 along Bay shore becomes 6 A.

1960: Last freight train runs.

Pier and marina completed.

1961: Cape Cod National Seashore made law by vote of U.S. congress.

1966: First true zoning bylaws, including 15,000 sq. ft. lot minimum lot size.

1974: First building inspector hired.

1975: Police department consists of 9 officers. Ratio of officers to population: 1 to 200.

1980s: Population finally surpasses that of the 1850 peak of 2411.

1986: Town switches to charter—traditional three fulltime selectmen replaced by five part-time, unpaid selectmen plus town administrator.

Wellfleet Cinemas in South Wellfleet open.

1987: Master Plan published, reflecting fears of consequences of unrestrained growth.

1988: Post Office moves from Main Street to Route 6.

1989: Library moves from Town Hall to present West Main St. location.

1990: Town dump becomes a transfer station; end of era of self- sufficient town trash disposal.

Local Comprehensive Plan, "Setting a Course For Our Future,"accepted by town meeting vote.

1997: First nonlocal building inspector hired.

1999: Land Bank passes, authorizing local taxation (with matching state funds) for purpose of buying lots for open space.

2000: 60 % of all houses belong to non-residents.

INTRODUCTION: CONFESSIONS OF A WASHASHORE

MOST OF THE PIECES included in this collection started life as columns for either the *Cape Cod Times*, for which I have been writing since 1994, or the *Provincetown Banner*, where I started in 1996. Anyone writing a column for a Cape Cod newspaper these days is aware, or ought to be, of having been preceded on the scene by Tom Kane ("Town Father"), whose column "My Pamet" appeared for decades in the *Cape Codder* and *Provincetown Advocate*. Kane started most pieces depicting himself emerging from his Truro home to read the "thin red line" of his thermometer, noting other features of the weather, expanding to local events, and ending with stories from the past. His voice epitomized a settled feeling about Truro and Wellfleet that, in the early and mid-1980s, connected me to the life of this place I was beginning to edge into, the life of those who had been here a long time and of the past they remembered. It seems to me that "My Pamet," although regularly anecdotal about the past, was not nostalgic in the wistful, elegiac way of more recent columns and books of grainy old photos and reminiscence of Olde Cape Cod. It was itself, having appeared since the 1940s, a river running out of the past into the present.

By the time I got the opportunity to write a column myself Tom Kane had died, the end of an era. Although

my editor at the *Cape Cod Times* urged pieces with an
Outer Cape flavor, I was not even for a second tempted
to try to do my own version of a "My Pamet." The most
obvious reason for this forbearance was that, as a recent
immigrant, I lacked the knowledge of—the embeddedness
in—the area, both the past and the present that was
Kane's starting point. But also it did seem that somewhere
around the time that Tom Kane stopped doing "My
Pamet," much as one wished he could have gone on doing
it forever, by sheer voice keeping the world of that Cape
alive, enough changes in that world had occurred,
threatening changes, that another sort of column seemed
called for, and one that didn't require the credential of
Kane's longtime residency. This narrowland has in recent
years become fraught, contentious terrain. Even as our
natural beauty and smalltown charm continue to be
celebrated (and acknowledged as a commodity by summer
visitors paying astounding rental rates), that settled,
peaceful quality of Tom Kane's Cape has been replaced by
a feeling of struggle—struggle, as I see it, for the soul of
this place. If Kane started each column reading the
thermometer and commenting on the weather, the
majority of my columns have started with my reading a
story in the paper about the latest threat to our quality of
life and commenting on the climate of opinion concerning
the issue.

ω ω ω

This perception of Wellfleet as struggling, stressed and
threatened is characteristic only of the most recent part of
my history with this town. Much of my experience of this
place over the years, like that of many washashores, has
been pure romance.

"Washashore" is what natives in these parts—and, I am
told, other coastal parts as well—call non-native residents.
There are worse things to be called than washashore. You

could be, and most of us were earlier in our evolution, a "summer complaint," the old term for varieties of summer people, part-time residents, summer renters, tourists and creatures still lower in the local hierarchy. In the big picture, washashore status is something of an achievement. Nevertheless there is in the term a bit of insult, an implication that, like the flotsam, jetsam, and driftwood that wash up on the beach, you occupy marginal space and might just wash away on the next tide.

This suggestion that the non-native resident usually lands in town by a process of aimless drifting on the currents of life, that he or she might just as easily have washed up on some other shore, certainly is not fair. Typically the non-native's choice as an adult to settle here is a result of considerable deliberation and experience both of this town and of others. It is, of course, natives that did not choose this town, although the adult native has exercised choice and commitment in remaining—or returning. If marriage to the town is the desirable, honorable conclusion, the washashore's is an adult marriage of love and commitment and the native's a marriage that at least starts as one made by the parents that may or may not turn into a relationship of commitment and affection.

But rootedness by birth, that which the washashore lacks by definition, is an important thing, a powerful sort of connectedness to a place that the washashore can only approximate by putting in the years. It has been pointed out to me that it is not through laziness or inadvertence that the cars of some residents—no doubt all washashores—display ten years of tattered dump and beach stickers. They are a sort of credential, evidence of tenure.

In any case, this washashore's story starts in the summer of 1959. I was planning to get married in September just before the start of my senior year in college. Someone suggested for a honeymoon destination a cute little town way out on Cape Cod named Wellfleet. I resisted this idea. No way I was going to join the crowds heading for Cape Cod, even back in those days a popular, bridge-clogging weekend destination. I had been doing preliminary work on a senior thesis on Thoreau and no doubt had a more austere, Thoreauvian retreat in mind (Thoreau with sex). Perhaps backpacking in the Maine woods, something like that. Certainly not a place made an instant cliché in a popular song by a singer named Patti Page.

I ended up going along with the Wellfleet suggestion only reluctantly, but the magic of the honeymoon merged with the charm of the beaches and the town and by the end of the week I was hooked. An old story with this place and, I imagine, with many another resort town. We slept the first night of our married life on the beach, an adventure which took on full, ironic meaning only many years later when I became aware that September 1959 was the very week legislation was introduced in Congress that would create the National Seashore park, one of the last moments in history one could legally, without hassle, camp on the beach.

After that first night we commuted from a guesthouse on Commercial Street to blissful days at the ocean. On the day we were scheduled to leave, a storm came and blew away summer, making it easier to leave. We returned to school and the first book I read for my Thoreau thesis was *Cape Cod*.

The marriage didn't take but the romance with Wellfleet got under my skin. There were occasional weekend pilgrimages in the '60s, and longish summer rentals with siblings and friends in the '70s (splitting $200 a week rent for an old, unwinterized Cape at the edge of a tidal marsh). In the late '70s my second (and, I trust, final) wife-to-be and I established a routine of tenting in the Audubon campground for a week in June and a week after Labor Day, in which the main activity was lounging all day at a particular pond. We still proudly display the citations for public nudity tendered by dutiful Seashore rangers during this period.

It was on one such visit in 1982 that, more or less on a whim (we had virtually no money), we decided to look around at building lots and were surprised to find that acquiring a piece of paradise was more or less affordable even for us. We borrowed the $6000 downpayment from my sister and bought one.

For several months over the next two summers and well into the fall, after over 20 years of tourist romance with this town I did my first real work here, building a small cabin on our one-plus acre lot in the woods. So lacking in neighbors were we back then that it felt comfortable living in a tent and then a small shed with no plumbing while working on the cottage. We worked slowly and self-indulgently, squeezing carpentry sessions in between sessions at beach and ponds, but it felt good to be no longer just a passive consumer of the town's pleasures but, in a small way, a producer.

In 1992, 33 years after my first visit, we finally achieved the status of washashore, moving here fulltime with our five-year-old son from the small, troubled New England city we had lived in for 17 years. We defended the move to our critical city friends, who tended to see us as rats abandoning the sinking ship by protesting that we were not fleeing the city but finally consummating a long courtship with a place that had all along felt like our true home. But it is true that our decision was given added urgency by the armed robbery of the convenience store at the end of our street and a murder down the block from where our toddler was being daycared, both in the final couple of years of our urban life.

It amazes even me that through all those tourist and part-time years I never once even considered defecting to any other Cape town, even for as little as a weekend. For me, from the beginning, there has never been any other

Cape Cod but Wellfleet. I assume this sort of chauvinism applies to devotees of other towns as well. Partisans of Brewster, Chatham or Orleans no doubt think it crazy to settle in the outer reaches of the Lower Cape, when you could be only a handy 20 minutes from the conveniences of Hyannis (and in the case of Orleans, boast several shopping plazas of your own). Trurovians (Trurorians? Truroites?), though they may make occasional use of Wellfleet's downtown are happy to be one stage more rural and avoid the possibility of summer season downtown congestion by the simple expedient of not having a downtown at all. Partisans of Provincetown probably wonder why anyone would bother driving all this distance from the mainland and not take the trouble to get to the natural destination, the very end of the road where the action is.

It was true, what we told our city friends on moving away: I always, since my first visit, thought of Wellfleet as a magically desirable place, an ideal, unattainable hometown. The small town I actually did grow up in the New York City suburbs had some of the layout and look of an All-American small town but lacked the basic logic and heart, being only a bedroom community for, and therefore an aspect of, Gotham. Wellfleet beckoned with the romance of the sea stories such as *Mutiny on the Bounty* or *Moby-Dick*, of Mark Twain's stories of boys on a large, exotic body of water. The secluded ponds with sandy bottoms and clear water reminded me of Thoreau's *Walden*. They were the swimmin' holes of American country lore missing from my actual hometown.

In a town with as long a history as a resort as this one, the romance can hardly be separated from the place. For summer visitors and other part-timers it is the quintessential experience of it. For washashores trailing long histories as part-timers the romance lives on as charming hangover. Probably even some natives get to believing the chamber of commerce hype and the echo of it in the rapturous compliments of summer people. There is a sense in which the romance, this infectious form of self-approval, is the way the town has come to think of itself.

Typical small towns—I think of towns lost in the vast anonymity of the non-coastal America—are, however loveable, not in love with themselves as this one is. The lack of self-consciousness, one could argue, makes them all the more loveable. Certainly, the image of our town we find most loveably charming is the one, glimpsed in old photos of fishermen and the clutter of a working waterfront or fully functioning, year-round Main Street, from the days early in the last century and before when Wellfleet was a more innocent, less self-conscious town.

Not long ago I taught a seminar in the literature of small towns in a series sponsored by the Wellfleet library. In re-reading such early 20th century classics as Sinclair Lewis's *Main Street* and Sherwood Anderson's *Winesburg, Ohio* I was surprised to be reminded just how negative and unromantic a view of small towns prevailed not so long ago. I can distinctly remember, in reading *Winesburg* and *Main Street* in my late teens, how sympathetic I was to the view that small towns—the smallness itself of small towns—were deadly to the spirit, especially the spirit of artistic temperaments such as the one I fancied I had. Such a view seemed at the time axiomatic: anybody with any energy or ambition (such as the Jimmy Stewart character in the movie *It's A Wonderful Life*) planned on shaking the dirt of that little nowhere burg off his shoes and going somewhere—usually a city—to pursue fame and fortune, or at least a more interesting life. Such were the negative, unromantic influences on my view of small towns not long before that first fling back in 1959 with the small town of Wellfleet. I have no recollection of having seen any irony in the contradiction.

ω ω ω

With our move here ten years ago the honeymoon begun in 1959 in a tent on the beach was over. My education in the reality of small towns, this small town, began. I think at first in some fuzzy way I thought that by choosing to live fulltime in this town we would be getting an even stronger dose of the romance of our part-time experience—isn't that too often the motive for marriage: fulltime access to the charms of the beloved? Real life here has of course proved otherwise.

Raising a child in a place is one sure cure for the disease of romance. Since we live only a third of a mile down a beautiful sand road from the elementary school, we imagined that our five year old, who started kindergarten the very week we moved, would walk every day down the sand road to school—perhaps, in season, barefoot, like Tom Sawyer; and surely the local teachers, being Wellfleet teachers, would approve. As it turned out he never once made that walk, barefoot or not. Refusing from the start to cooperate with our romantic vision, he chose to walk up to the paved road to catch the bus for that two-minute ride, his motives bodily ease and social opportunity.

If I had expected the school to be some magical Wellfleet version of an elementary school, with Wellfleetian teachers and a Wellfleetian educational theory (or rather lack of theory, that being more consistent with the local self-image), as magically different from other schools as I imagined the town was from all ordinary towns, then I soon joined the ranks of the disillusioned. It seemed a very good school—but a school. Most of the teachers had been educated in standard methodology and didn't even live here but in up-Cape towns hereabouts thought of as tending dangerously toward the suburban.

Building is another vital entry into the real workings of a town—having a reason to go to Town Hall other than purchase beach stickers, making oneself known in the lumberyard. But beyond that it involves an essential loss of innocence. New construction can be thought of as one of the cardinal sins of this time of threatened resources and overcrowding. If so, it is a sin I have committed—and not just by hiring others to do the dirty work, but with my own hands.

Probably the most telling sign of having washed ashore is a shift of emphasis from natural scenery to the human scene. For many years this place of Wellfleet meant primarily its natural setting—ocean, ponds, woods, marshes. The town itself, though charming, was primarily a launching pad for adventures in nature. I gather this is true for most who visit here. Looking back over my years as a part-timer, it is remarkable how well-hidden the town and its people were behind the scenery. I knew a lot about the ponds, the routes to the more secluded ones, paths to unpeopled stretches of ocean beach; I knew remarkably little about the real life of this town. But it didn't take long at all into our first autumn before I began to know and care about what went on inside those buildings known to me for so long only as facades: meetings at the library Monday nights and in the Town Hall basement on Wednesday nights, the lunch special season at the two year-round restaurants, the location of the floating coffee hangout (when there was one), the bootleg pizza in the middle of winter, Town Meetings or rec games in the school gym. If someone had been keeping count he would have noted that gradually key terms in our Wellfleet vocabulary such as *Dyers* or *Spectacle, Newcomb to the left, the isthmus* had to move over and make room for *pot-luck, the hole, warrant article, charter,* ZBA, Conscom, *Fincom* and that constant refrain, *community.*

ω ω ω

Writing regularly about this place for local newspapers has been one of my more intense experiences of the limits of romance. Tom Kane, in his farewell column in 1989, wrote: "I have tried over the years to keep my column

non-political and inoffensive to all of my fellow citizens."
While I don't even aspire to the goal of being non-
political, I, too, have tried to be as inoffensive as possible
while still digging into the issues, most of which can be
discussed without pointing a finger at specific fellow
citizens. (I notice I am more likely to advertise the name
of an up-Cape developer or representative of a large
corporation come to town to talk us into something than
the protagonists in a strictly local controversy.)

Nevertheless, one may give offense once in a while
despite inoffensive intentions, as I found out early on in
my column-writing career. I was being interviewed by the
selectmen for a position on a town committee when one
of the interviewers started by saying: "Why do you hate
this town so much?" She had read a column ("At Home
with Entropy," 1994) in which I describe the
unpretentious charms of what would elsewhere be called
eyesores. I was sure the fondness of my irony would be
clear to all readers; in fact my romantic identification with
this town was still in its monolithic stage in which I
assumed all whom this town had touched shared one soul,
that we were all one citizenry—Wellfleet people—
characterized among others things by both irony and a
taste for the unpretentious and even the rundown. But
here was one of my fellow citizens, a native as a matter of
fact, with one of those names one sees on street signs,
who obviously didn't appreciate or understand my way of
being fond of this town.

My own mother used to give us the advice "if you can't
say something nice, don't say anything at all," so I suppose
I have only myself to blame for a response to a column a
few years back. I wrote, despite having little nice to say,
about a man who, in a town just off-Cape, had shot his
ex-girlfriend's current boyfriend, raped her, and then shot
himself. The real point of the piece was to criticize the
role played in the tragedy by the tendency of our society
to glamorize violent men. The morning this column ap-

peared I answered the phone and was assaulted by the opening line, "What is this ---- you wrote, you -------?" It was an Outer Cape example of one of those violent men I had been talking about, objecting, as far as I could make out through the abuse, to my call for de-glamorizing his kind. My mother also used to say, "sticks and stones will break my bones but words will never hurt me" (which seems to mean roughly the opposite of the other advice). Apparently the words in my column had hurt this guy enough that if I ever actually met him in the flesh it would be sticks and stones I'd have to worry about.

On the other hand there was the time I was jogging past the lumberyard when a woman employee with whom I had hitherto had only friendly over-the-counter business dealings ran out and waylaid me with a hug—my reward for having written a column ("The Implied Ocean," '97) that struck her in just the right way.

Some writers might find the small town situation—the likelihood that you will be coming face-to-face with your readership as well as your subject matter—a straitjacket; I find it a wholesome discipline. However these essays come across to others, I can say that when I am doing them I feel very much a citizen writing *in medias res*: from within this town, caught up in our history. And I take that as a good thing.

It has felt like a real privilege to have the opportunity to write about this place that has meant so much to me for so long, even if by the time I came to write about it, much of the time it has meant writing less about the garden of one's romance than the snake in that garden. I am convinced that what happens to this town—the outcome of the struggle for its soul—matters. And not only to the town itself; in a world in which the forces of economic and cultural globalization seem to be carrying the day, we are an endangered species. There is something in this cherished, threatened place that is worth speaking up for.

ESSENTIAL REGIONAL TERMINOLOGY

OURS IS A REGION DISTINGUISHED, among other ways, by its preoccupation with regional and sub-regional distinctions. Regional terminology is an essential part of the experience of living here.

Cape Cod has traditionally been divided into Upper Cape and Lower Cape, with more recently a Mid-Cape thrown in. To the uninitiated, the Lower/Upper metaphor may call up misleading images of topographical verticality or latitude (as in "up north," "down south"), or even the suggestion of moral stratification (higher nature, lower impulses, etc.). Our Lower/Upper is actually, as far as I know, drawn from the region's seagoing past, specifically from the prevailing wind direction so important to sailors. Up-Cape is upwind, in the direction of the prevailing westerlies, or west of the speaker. Down-Cape is downwind or easterly of the speaker. Upper Cape is the westerly part, Lower Cape is the easterly part. (The same nautical metaphor is found in Martha's Vineyard's "upisland" and "downisland" and Maine's "downeast.")

Down is east—in theory, anyway. In actuality, as you drive towards Provincetown, past the Orleans-Eastham rotary, down-Cape refers no longer to east but, by turns, to north, northwest, and finally, in Provincetown's convolutions, west, thus doing a literal 180 with the original sense of "down"—all without a U-turn on your part.

But the usefulness of the Upper/Lower Cape dichotomy to the residents of the Lower Cape town of Wellfleet is compromised even more by its inclusiveness. Even with the upstart term "Mid-Cape" (annoying in its disregard of the traditional nautical metaphor underlying its companion terms), taking up territory that traditionally belonged to "Lower-" and "Upper-", Lower Cape, in including Orleans, Brewster, Chatham and Harwich as it usually does, feels too inclusive to be used for the sub-Cape region of which most Wellfleetians feel themselves to be a part. I believe there is a shared feeling here that whatever our region or sub-region is, it stops short of Orleans.

This is no doubt partly because of the malls and other suburban features that have transformed Orleans in the past few decades. Ironically it may be just the fact that we depend on Orleans for our serious shopping that excludes it from our sub-region.

Nauset is a good local native-American name used traditionally for much of this area and now appropriated for the regional school district to which Wellfleet belongs. But it seems not to have succeeded in getting locals to enlarge our sense of our region to include the other Lower Cape towns of the school district. Instead, Wellfleet parents' oft-expressed annoyance with the amount of time our children must spend on the bus getting to the middle school in Orleans suggests that the region is just too large to feel like ours.

Since, for various reasons, Lower Cape is too inclusive a term, and perhaps, for unnautical moderns, just too confusing, the more exclusive term Outer Cape has gained favor for the part of the Lower Cape consisting of Provincetown, Truro, Wellfleet and Eastham, which seem for most of us to compose the region we think of as ours. The prevailing westerlies in relation to which we are "lower" prevail only when the weather is good. During a nor'easter, the wind is from one point of east or another, and then those of us huddling behind the dunes of the ocean beach are upwind of everyone else. Rather than "lower" we feel "outer," as in: way out here, taking the brunt.

"Outer" is expressive of both our geographical and our cultural distance from the bridges which connect the Cape to the rest of the country. If all the Cape, in projecting so far out into the sea, turns its back on America, as Thoreau said, we beyond the elbow in his arm image of the Cape are the farthest out—far enough out to be farout, in the 'sixties counterculture sense—and proudly use this term in names such as Beston's famous Outermost House and Outermost Radio, WOMR-FM.

Another concept associated with our region, narrowness, is thematically related to our outer-ness and "narrowland" is another favored way of referring to this place. If all the Cape is narrow, with connotations of leanness and spareness, compared to the corpulent mainland, because we are farther out we are also narrower, and because narrower, more exposed to the elements, wilder. The whole idea of the Cape is narrowness, and we are the narrowest of the narrow. I am using "we" loosely here, I realize. To Provincetown folks no doubt Eastham and Wellfleet have an almost midwestern expansiveness to them.

Around here, the narrower the better, to the point, I suppose, where the quintessential cross section of Outer Cape would be a two-edged beach with bay and Atlantic waters lapping away at both sides. Shades of Wellfleet's Billingsgate Island in its latter days, high tide waters of bay and harbor (if not ocean) mingling around the ankles of the diehard patrons astride their barstools of the last Billingsgate tavern.

AT HOME WITH ENTROPY

FOR A TOWN KNOWN for its picturesqueness, Wellfleet has its share of what most of the world would count as eyesores: houses with flaking paint, houses with ragged shingles, houses with rotting porches. A storefront slapped onto the front of an old Greek revival.

In a climactic spot at the harbor where one might expect to find Architecture saluting the view, we have the asbestos shingle-and-plywood-sided hodgepodge that houses our theater and locals' coffee break hangout. Down the beach from this, to put it kindly, low-key structure is a miscellany of summer cottages in various states of disrepair that seem all but oblivious of their location front row center on Wellfleet's Gold Coast.

Our indispensable pizza joint is housed in a structure that deviates alarmingly from the vertical, mocking the whole notion of a building code. (I must say the owner, in choosing a name, showed remarkable restraint in resisting the obvious pun on the out-of-kilter Italian tower.) Our famous town footbridge, Uncle Tim's, recently the subject of a huge photo on the front page of the *New York Times* travel section, features unfinished, twisted, split and apparently life-threatening railings. The margins of the harbor are littered with the decaying hulls of derelict fishing boats, some reduced to the rusting engine block.

One could go on.

If fighting the good fight against the insidious forces of entropy is the hallmark of a solid bourgeoisie, then we are, I am afraid, letting down the home side. But of course it is to be understood that, while these features might be considered unsightly and substandard in some places, they are what passes for charming here. Exposure to the elements being the name of the game in this narrow land, we prefer our buildings to show the effects of that exposure. A freshly installed shingle, raw and yellowish, just doesn't look right until it has learned humility before the weather. Gray is the color of that lesson. Likewise, the fate of paint is to flake. We paint when we must to protect our investment, but pre-emptive maintenance smacks of hubris. We would rather embrace an aesthetic of which getting run down becomes the very essence. Our rural blight is our scenery.

If the town is charming, that is owing more to the weather and passage of time than to architects. Architecture—especially the more recent stuff ambitious to exploit the water view—is more likely to be seen as blocking the scenery than celebrating it. The fact is, Uncle Frank's harborside coffee place would be uncomfortable—inconceivable—in a building even vaguely associated with architecture. It seems possible that Wellfleet Harbor Actors' Theater would have failed to develop its reputation for outrageous theater in a more dignified setting.

I don't know for a fact that rigorous application of the building code and flavor in pizza have an inverse relationship, but it seems a distinct possibility. It is, in any case, hard to imagine the author of this particular pizza producing or his patrons as happily consuming it in a more competent setting.

There simply are no eyesores in this town, no blight, no architectural vacuum (or even architecture) that cannot be turned into scenery by a few years' exposure to driven salt rain, sleet, snow, blown sand and gravity (all nurtured by benign neglect); or, failing all else, by the sheer determination of the faithful to perceive everything hereabouts as picturesque.

THE KINDNESS
OF STRANGERS

YOU CAN SEE THEM crowding the aisles of the downtown grocery on weekends, inflicting their business on the poor owner, who for the past seven months has enjoyed almost total solitude at this hour.

Oh, you can tell who they are, the casualness of their dress falling well short of the local standard for slovenliness.

I'm amazed, having washed ashore here myself a mere two years ago after three decades as a more-or-less seasonal devotee, at how easy it is to get into this we/them, anti-tourist thing. Sporting at the expense of the plague of tourists and other part-timers seems as necessary to conversation in these parts as wry humor about the weather.

We need a little perspective on this xenophobia. After all, not only did a rather high percentage of current residents arrive in the recent past; the town's Founding Fathers and Mothers themselves floated here clad in outlandish costumes from places farther away than Boston or New Jersey. (Of course, in the view of some, you can't get farther from the Cape than New Jersey.)

Even the Cape itself is a johnny-come-lately tourist of sorts, having been plowed up here by a pushy glacier from the north. With no roots in the bedrock, it is a here-today-gone-tomorrow phenomenon in geological terms.

Anti-tourist sentiment is based on the widely indulged belief that the Cape was better off before the era of tourism. The first two and a half centuries of settlement, the period of farming, fishing and whaling, was the Great Period from which we have degenerated. Tourism is a form of that degeneration, the mode of our decline and fall.

But in our romancing of the indigenous we should not forget that the old-timers did their share of trashing this fragile place, clear-cutting trees to feed their fires and conduct their business, overgrazing with the resultant loss of topsoil to the point where they worried about sand actually clogging the waterways. By as early as the end of the 18th century, the Outer Cape had been turned into a virtual wasteland. Being Old Wellfleet was no guarantee of virtue.

Neither is full-time residency. In our own time, tourists and the second-home market may provide the motivation for the construction of the malls and housing developments that have so changed the character of the Cape, but the actual perpetrators in many cases are our own home-grown developers and builders.

On the other hand, visitors have done much to preserve the Cape. Two of the most famous names associated with the Outer Cape, the Henrys Thoreau and Beston, were hardly more than day-trippers and yet they were, most would agree, true citizens in the spiritual sense.

The National Seashore Park, appreciated now as a great preserver of the quality of life hereabouts, was widely opposed by residents and pushed through only by such outsiders as the Kennedys and the federal government.

The same could be said of some other natural treasures. Yosemite and the rest of the Sierra Nevada owe a great deal to such part-timers as John Muir and other Sierra Club weekend hikers.

Thoreau's sojourn at Walden was possibly the single most important event in the history of that pond. That famous stay and the classic he wrote about it have been indispensable in preserving what is now seen by many as a sacred site—not from other pilgrims and tourists but from developers and other full-time residents with designs.

Sheer numbers of bodies is very definitely a concern in this era of this narrow land. One of the qualities of life here has always been a relative remoteness and spaciousness and every new body is a dilution of that quality—even if the body is that of a poet or a worshipful tourist.

But another quality of our life is a shared sense of this being a sacred, cherished landscape. Visitors, and not just artists but garden-variety tourists, simply by loving it here, have done much to enhance this quality.

THE MUSEUMIFICATION
OF UNCLE TIM
AND AUNT SALLY

I NOTICE THERE'S A SPIFFY NEW SIGN next to Uncle Tim's bridge informing anyone who didn't already know that in fact it is Uncle Tim's bridge. This rickety footbridge crosses Duck Creek and leads to picturesque walks along the inner harbor shore.

Uncle Tim's is one of Wellfleet's most hallowed landmarks, an ancient tradition hereabouts. As such, it didn't really need a sign. It was its own best sign and, as perhaps our architectural feature most favored by artists, kind of a sign of Wellfleet.

Actually, there was a sign there already, a little metal thing. This sign was also superfluous, but stylistically unambitious and sufficiently faded and dented to blend in. It no longer stood apart from what it named, and so had ceased, in a sense, to be a sign. Perhaps that is why the new sign was commissioned. It's hard to believe that anyone not objecting to the weatherbeaten, unkempt look of the bridge itself would have sicced the town officials on the old sign on aesthetic grounds.

The last time I thought to look, the old sign was still there. Perhaps it blended in so successfully that the installers of the new sign decided it was part of the scenery and didn't need to come down. In which case the new sign should read:

UNCLE TIM'S BRIDGE AND OLD UNCLE TIM'S SIGN

The style of the new sign is the problem. In its fancy Chippendale curve at the top and fresh blue and white paint there is just the hint of an implication that perhaps the bridge itself, with its ancient tarred pilings, the brittle, twisted railings, and total innocence of paint, should be remodelled to look more like something suitable for a suburban miniature golf course.

It makes me nervous when the powers-that-be start paying this sort of homage to local features. Next thing you know, the traditional year-round restaurant on Main Street, in addition to its business sign will get its blue-and-white sign officially declaring it to be:

LIGHTHOUSE RESTAURANT

If Uncle Tim's picturesqueness gets to be officially acknowledged as such, surely the wrecked boat hulls left to rot in the marshy edges of the harbor deserve official blessing:

ROTTING BOAT HULLS AND RUSTING ENGINE BLOCKS

For that matter, why not call attention to our colorful residents as essential features of the local scene?

AUNT SALLY SITTING ON HER PORCH

JANE, FULL-TIME RESIDENT AND WAITRESS

TOBY, BELOVED TOWN MONGREL

HOME OF DICK, TOWN CHARACTER, WITH COLORFULLY BEAT-UP PICKUP IN DRIVEWAY

TOWN MEETING WITH CITIZENS EXERCISING RIGHTS

Wellfleet has resisted more successfully than a lot of tourist towns the almost irresistible urge to package its picturesqueness, museumify its quaintness. After over 100 years of tourism we are hardly unconscious of our charms, but we have evolved a happy practice of not exploiting them unduly; in fact, relative unselfconsciousness can be said to be one of our charms.

I'm not really worried about this new Uncle Tim's sign. I expect that, being a Wellfleet sign and not a Chatham or Orleans sign, it will begin to weather and peel within a relatively short time in accordance with our unofficial town policy of design by attrition.

VARIETIES
OF
HUMAN INTERVENTION

ONE DAY A FEW YEARS AGO I jogged along a sand road to one of my favorite ponds, hidden deep in the woods. I discovered that since my last pilgrimage this sweet little pond, which had simply been there minding its own business for, presumably, some millennia, had finally been blessed with official notice from the great world beyond. Here, in demure National Seashore brown and white were a box of helpful Pond Guides and a sign listing ecologically correct Pond Regulations. And, replacing a low and sometimes wet section of the path leading to the pond's edge, a boardwalk.

I had entertained no illusions that this was my secret, wild pond. You can drive the road I jogged; there is a small, sandy parking space. The pond had long served the community as an unofficial skinny-dipping spot. But while the pond was regularly visited by those in the know, there seemed to be an unspoken agreement to think of it as a secret-in-common, a treasured community asset buried in the woods. Now, with this official notice, however well-meaning, the community secret had been exposed, banalized, unearthed. . . polluted.

The new sign instructed us not to use the pond as a bathtub or urinal. No doubt the pond, although pristine in appearance, is not innocent of the occasional pollution by rank swimming dog or toddler urine. I had once, years before, felt compelled to play the heavy and object to some teenagers using soap to bathe. I certainly believe in the need to pay careful attention to how we behave in such places.

And yet there was something about this particular form of attention bestowed by the Seashore powers-that-be that disturbed me. For one thing, it ignored a long history of people just naturally caring for this beautiful little pond—using it and not abusing it. I wondered if anyone involved with the decision to intervene here had nearly as much history with this site as those of us who have on the whole lovingly used it through the years. It was hard to believe that anyone who had actually spent much time there would have so violated the spirit of the place.

The boardwalk had apparently been installed to correct what someone in charge had perceived as a problem: people creating alternative routes to avoid wet feet when the main path to the pond got mushy. The alternative path had been there as far as I could remember, and I had done my part in maintaining it by using it occasionally. I never blamed myself or others for seeking to keep our feet dry. Even if it did squash a few plants, the bypass struck me as having the pleasingly simple, human logic of most paths and doing much less to impose itself on the setting than the boardwalk itself (constructed, of course, of wood treated with poison, since anything else would rot out in short order). A prime case of the medicine being worse than the disease.

How, I wondered, had the Seashore arrived at the decision to intervene here? Had an actual habitue of the pond, feet still muddy, called them to ask that something be done? Had some federal Theorist of the Wild extrapolated from that one alternative path to a scenario in which the entire park would be trampled flat by people trying to keep their shoes dry?

I have heard the term "sign pollution" and I guess it applies here, even if this sign says, essentially, "don't pollute." The abstract, ahistorical, noncommunal feeling communicated by so many bureaucratic actions is itself a form of pollution.

One morning this past summer when I jogged to this same pond and was congratulating myself on having it all to myself I found someone had erected in a few feet of water a graceful circle of slender reeds perhaps ten feet in diameter. Aha. Someone else has been here, left a calling card. According to an article in the newspaper I read later, sculptor Roy Staab had chosen my pond as a venue for Art. At the same time that I felt a loss of intimacy at the pond's becoming a media star, it was also flattering. Certainly no pond was more deserving of such an honor.

Our National Seashore authorities took swift and decisive action, ordering the perpetrator to remove the offending construction forthwith. One of the problems was that, however appropriate it seemed aesthetically to the setting, it was made of nonindigenous materials— reeds from the harbor side of town, and string. Further, as any fool could plainly see, it was not "natural." Being a work of art, it in fact positively reeked of playful human creativity. Clearly, it had to go.

And yet I must say, when it comes to forms of human intervention, I much prefer the reed sculpture to the park's own touches.

COYOTES
OUT OF CONTEXT

IN THIS LAND WHERE OTHER SPECIES are almost as likely as we are to make the headlines, we have a new media personality. The usual suspects—those whales and dolphins and exotic turtles that are always getting themselves stranded on the flats—have been upstaged in recent weeks by another sort of exotic washashore, the coyote.

There are stories in the paper about the dog officer who is sure she was attacked by one (even if that would make her one of only a handful of victims in recorded history, or so we are told), the Truro man feeling threatened to the point of shooting one. There is spirited debate in the papers about just what attitude we ought to take toward these interlopers.

Now I know we ought, in these days of threatened wilderness, to be grateful for anything wild that comes our way. Nevertheless, I have mixed feelings the advent of these scrawny canines. In my youth a coyote howling from a distant ridge (the cowpokes hunkered down around the campfire) was a symbol of the wild frontier. However it was for the kids growing up in the actual West, to a kid from this coast a coyote was a beast from the Wild West mythology of the movies.

It was that filmic background that made it a particular thrill when, camping in the '60s with friends in the Sierra

Nevada mountains of California, hunkered down around our own campfire, we heard, in the pauses in conversation, that same yipping in the night from a distant ridge. Wow, you hear that? Far out. Wild. Really wild.

I had gone West ostensibly to attend graduate school but subtextually, like any American boy, like Lewis and Clark, Davy Crockett, Jack Kerouac and others guys before me, to put my body in the actual landscape of the myth. One of the first things I did on arriving in that exotic land was to check out the implication in the popular Kingston Trio song about the "wild coast" of Big Sur that by the '60s there were no more mountain lions. Talk about an exotic, mythical animal, with its feline cousins in the jungles of tropical Americas, Africa and Asia. I was told in no uncertain terms I had arrived too late. The big cats—those that hadn't gotten themselves caged in zoos or stuffed in museums—had split the scene decades before.

But if we couldn't have mountain lions (or grizzlies, or wolves), at least here were these wild ur-dogs to put one in touch with the Ancient Mysteries. Look Ma, here I am sharing space with coyotes!

I at length finished school and settled for a job Back East, as I had learned to think of it (the "back" always carrying a a bit of the connotation of retreat as the "out" of Out West did of adventure, risk). I bid a fond farewell to the wild coast and the land of the coyote. Eventually I ended up here on the tame coast.

And here are those coyotes poking around my backyard (as it were; I haven't actually seen one yet) in one of the more settled areas in the country. I know how I got here. What I want to know is: How did they get here, from that high Sierra ridge and wild west mythology to the everyday life here in the civilized? How did they cross all those interstates? How did they cross the cultivated plains of the Midwest, penetrate the wall-to-

32

wall backyards and megalopolises of the East? Why did they? How are they handling the culture shock?

And how did they make it across the bridges? Can you picture them hiding in the bushes in back of the Friendly's at the Sagamore rotary until the traffic died down late at night and then marching single file across under strict orders not to howl at the moon lest they attract unwanted attention?

This coyote comeback certainly is interesting, but when you come down to it, I'd rather wild critters stuck to the appropriately wild settings where I had them mentally stashed. Having them right here on Page three of my local newspaper and competing with the racoons for the garbage doesn't really make the Cape seem any wilder. And it dilutes the wildness of the coyote.

ROOTING FOR CHAOS

I AM WRITING THIS in the early moments of a much ballyhooed storm. One of the TV channels has been calling it The Nor'easter of '95—although that may say more about media desperation in a mostly boring winter than about this storm.

When I first woke at 6 a.m. the trees in dim light were motionless. The storm had been predicted to hit early. This was the calm before, I guessed. Soon the wind began to stir and now, three hours later, after a tentative flake or two, the snow is coming down in earnest. No, that sober-citizen image doesn't do it. This snow is coming down with abandon. Better get up the driveway to retrieve the paper while I can still find it.

Even though I have gone about my early morning business more or less as usual, I have been aware of the energy rising in me as the wind rises in the trees. The ancient feeling, going right back to early childhood: storm coming, big storm. This will not be a normal day. Best laid plans of mice and men about to get mislaid bigtime.

This excitement is partly media-generated. I have seen Ohio being snowed upon by a version of this very storm. I have seen the diagram of the computer's thinking: the low from the Midwest ganging up with the low over the ocean "should explode off Cape Hatteras and move right up over Cape Cod." But I have also been informed that because it will move over Cape Cod and not farther out to sea our snow will turn to rain within a few hours. Thus, this snow, even in its most pristine moment, is already tainted by the forecast of the slush it will become. How different it must have been when blizzards did not piggyback on a blizzard of media hype.

A lot of us are romantics when it comes to storms— probably more on Cape Cod than in the general population; don't we move out here at least in part to expose ourselves to storms? One aspect of romanticism is identifying with the natural violence to the point of, in effect, rooting against your own kind, against yourself. It is a form of decadence only societies of a certain stage of development can afford to indulge.

My father—by the time I knew him, anyway—did not fancy storms. He took a clear stand against them, seeing in them only inconvenience, paths to be shoveled, higher coal bills. When I was in high school he badly fractured his leg slipping on an icy sidewalk on his way home from work, thus corroborating his prejudice against the Winter Wonderland, as the popular song of the time was calling it.

Temporary inmate as I was, I had no stake in my father's house, his projects, his worries. I was all on the side of the storm, rooting for it against him, against us. A hurricane or ice storm or blizzard was only serious if it did damage. I remember trying to work out the contradiction: You didn't want people to die, of course, but the fact is the "death toll" was one of the more thrilling measures of the strength of the storm. I have kept track of this romantic betrayal of my species in the thrill of a storm and have noticed it seriously eroding with homeownership. I have acquired a certain amount of sympathy for my father's Scrooge-like failure to get into the spirit of things.

We are told that until fairly recently, for the first two centuries or so of European settlement, the Outer Cape's storm-facing "back side" was a place associated with terrible dangers to seamen, the abode of demons, a howling wilderness. Not a place sensible, God-fearing people would build a house, unless hunkered down in a hollow. Perhaps not a view they found pleasant, even on a fair day, so clearly was this ocean the enemy (even if economic survival required wresting things of value from its grasp). Even today it's a good guess that the most likely victims of ferocious weather—residents of the Carolinas' Outer Banks or our own fishermen who put out to sea in small boats—are less inclined to indulge in this storm romance, even as a minority report from the depths of the soul.

These days when technology has nature on the ropes, the TV anchors don't even try very hard to conceal their own storm romanticism, presumably shared by the audience. Oh, there are the sober warnings, the annual explanation of anatomically correct shoveling technique, the reports as if from a war front. But bubbling up through the show of sobriety, a veritable orgy of snow depths, closings, reports of accidents, havoc wreaked. The basic feeling is that we can afford to entertain the storm as an uncouth but interesting guest and enjoy the excuse for a bit of vacation from business as usual.

NIPPING PROGRESS IN THE BUD

IT SEEMED TO THE SELECTMEN a nice bit of progress, the proposed upscaling of the bus stop in front of town hall. Replace an old, cracked sidewalk with a new brick patio; a tired, old tree with two eager new ones. At the same time create a turnout to get the bus out of the way of stampeding tourists. No hearing was considered necessary. Such obvious improvement, and at no cost to the town, since grant money was available. Who could object?

A lot of people, as it turned out.

One citizen read the small print in the official announcements in the paper, showed up at the selectmen's meeting to find the application for the bus stop grant money already a *fait accompli*. But she spoke spiritedly for the tree, hugged it afterwards for the photographer from a local paper, circulated petitions that eventually collected 250 signatures. Who could object to this clear bit of progress for the town? Turns out just about everyone who heard about it and was not riding out the winter on a tropical beach had feelings about the matter.

In the face of such a show of passion for the arboreal status quo, the selectmen changed their mind and withdrew the application for money.

What is the meaning of this moment of small-town history? What is this besides sheer, ornery resistance to progress? Paradoxically this resistance to progress represents progress—in consciousness. A moment of heightened awareness, of values clarification. A contribution to a new definition of progress.

The same kind of progressive consciousness is being applied up-Cape in the outpouring of resistance to the double-barreling of the Mid-Cape Highway. A highway not widened. A bus stop not upgraded. Progress. Progress is not always doing something. Sometimes it is resisting doing something. (Don't just do something—stand there!)

Too often conservation/preservation is reduced, often by developers or other profiteers seeking to usurp the high ground, to clinging to the past for its own sake, putting it before the needs of the present and future. It will represent real progress if we can begin to see that it is, on the contrary, a fight precisely for the quality of life of those living, not a museumfication of the town. A lot of us, if not some of the selectmen, are fond of the front of town hall as it is: that old tree, that funky sidewalk and benches, the bus stop just a no-fuss, no-bother pause in town. There is fondness for the familiar in this preference, yes, but other values as well: modesty, simplicity, restraint. Important human values, I would say, for a culture spinning out of control.

Real progress would be recognition, especially on the part of those who undertake to make decisions about the town's future, that such modesty and restraint are part and parcel of the charm and soul of this town and as such its real assets (if one wants to get bottom-line about it).

We ought to know from our appreciation of this town that not all that is slow should be made fast. Not all that is small should be made big. Not all that is unpainted should be painted. Sand should not always be paved.

Not all that is simple should be made complex. Not all that is old should be thrown out in favor of something young. Improvements don't always improve things. Development is very often mis-development. Progress is often regress.

More efficient is not always better. Higher tech is not always better tech. Not all lots that can be built on should be built on. Not all pretty little tourist towns should become Aspen or the Hamptons.

A lot of residents, part-time residents and tourists are very fond of this town. But we have a history of not always being clear enough about what we value to know when it is being threatened. The post office got moved to Route 6 despite hearings that seemed overwhelmingly in favor of keeping it as a focal point of social life on Main Street. The National Seashore, which institutionalized the virtues of fallowness on the Lower Cape 30-some years ago, met with widespread local opposition.

And 40 years ago paving won the battle in Wellfleet, and what got paved was not just a bit of town hall lawn but the best of the waterfront. A delicate spit of sand called, winningly, Shirttail Point, was buried under five acres of blacktop—our town pier. Would that that desecration in the name of progress had been nipped in the bud by the kind of clarity that has prevailed in the matter of the bus stop.

TWO-THIRDS EMPTY GLASS

APRIL IS THE CRUELEST MONTH, I have always supposed, because in the climatologically challenged regions we share with the poet it teases with the prospect of good weather. Outer Cape Codders know to expect nothing of March, even if it contains the official start of spring. But of April we have definite expectations.

Since April got us thinking once again, however April foolishly, about the possibility of good weather, it seems timely to ask: Just what constitutes good weather, anyway? And how much of it do we get in a typical year? Now by "good weather" I don't mean weather that provides the occasion for the pleasurable exercise of irony and satire (much as I personally appreciate the many opportunities for such exercise with which we are blessed year-round). Or weather that provides overtime for snowplow drivers or extra profits for the fuel companies; yeah, I know, it's an ill wind....and so on, but that's not what I'm talking about.

By "good" I certainly don't mean "interesting" or "stimulating" weather of the sort New England specializes in. The fact is a certain significant percent of our days, while they may be interesting as hell, puts a significant percent of us in the mood for oversleeping, overeating, doubling up on our Prozac dosage or hours spent in bars. I am willing to go out on a limb and call such weather bad weather, in the sense of daunting to the body and spirit.

Good weather is what's left over.

In an earlier column I alluded to the "two-thirds empty glass of New England weather." If this bit of surliness was admittedly a shot from the hip (weather influenced, no doubt), then just how full or empty is our meteorological glass? Towards a comfort quotient, I offer the following suggestions of standards:

*The pocketbook-derived definition of good weather would be WEATHER WARM ENOUGH THAT WE DON'T NEED TO HEAT OUR HOMES. June, July, August and September, with maybe another month's worth of days culled from May and October, yielding perhaps five months—a 40 percent full glass.

*One could reasonably argue that the good weather portion of the year is the period in which we can take inspiration from FULL FLOURISHING OF PLANT LIFE, a period of four months, max. A one-third full glass.

*The Cape being a watery sort of place, we might define good weather as the SWIMMING SEASON. Taking a pond temperature of 68 as a measure of swimmable (there are those who would claim it is always winter at the Outer Cape ocean), that yields about four months for the reasonably hardy. Of course, the unreasonably hardy would want to claim May and October, beefing up the season to six months. On the other hand, may I point out that when trying to find a truly comfortable swimming temperature at which to set pool thermostats, we choose the low 80s, precisely the winter temperature of the Caribbean, but a temperature never even approached in these deprived regions. A one-third full glass.

*At the other end of the water-pegged continuum, fishermen, for all I know, define good weather as THAT

PERIOD OF THE YEAR WHEN IF YOU FALL OUT OF YOUR BOAT YOU DON'T FREEZE TO DEATH IN UNDER FIVE MINUTES. They would be rewarded for their modest expectations with perhaps an eight-month season, a two-thirds full glass.

*How about WARMER THAN THE REFRIGERA-TOR as a standard? It always seems to me absurdly masochistic that those of us who have strayed into these dubious latitudes subject ourselves to a climate in which a big chunk of the year approximates that of the mini-morgues we maintain to preserve the flesh of fellow creatures destined as meals. About nine months of the year average above the refrigerator temperature of 40 degrees. A three-fourths full glass.

*My own candidate for the most profound definition of good weather: WEATHER FRIENDLY TO OUR SPECIES. That is, weather more or less like that which was a necessary condition to our development as the sort of hairless creature we are: weather warm enough to wear little or no clothes outdoors, the weather found in abundance in the aforementioned Caribbean but hereabouts only in the warmest months, June through September. Very optimistically, a quarter-filled glass.

No doubt someone will argue that since it has been in our species' nature to innovate such things as down jackets and furnaces and hot mulled wine we are only truly comfortable when the weather is such that we get to use such devices. That we would rather be clever than comfortable. That, I suppose, it isn't really natural for us to be natural.

But such considerations would send us spinning completely out of the happy little universe of this column.

REQUIEM
FOR SHIRTTAIL POINT

WELLFLEET'S TOWN PIER is the mother of all smalltown piers. (Let that colorful, if overused, Saddamism, the mother of all hyperboles, qualify this as my Mom's Day column.)

Measuring 150 by 1,500 feet, it is a five-acre mesa of blacktop dominating the harbor. There are finger-piers running the length of the more sheltered side of it, a boat launching ramp on the other. But decades after it was finished it still is mostly just a gigantic parking lot in search of a mall. It has, according to one town guide, a capacity of 640 cars, and could serve to relieve the summer parking crush downtown, half a mile away. But being half a mile away, it doesn't. My impression is that it is rarely as much as a quarter filled with cars and most of the time is an asphalt desert.

I've lived more or less at peace with that vast rectangle of pavement for the 35 years of my acquaintance with this town. It's always just been there, a familiar feature of the landscape, like a familiar relative to a kid, too big and too close to wrap your vision around, to form a judgment about. A given.

Recently, I came across a 1940s USGS topographical map which shows what the inner harbor looked like not so long before my time. It turns out that buried under our aircraft carrier-sized pier is the delicate, sinuous sandbar graphically named Shirttail Point. Photos displayed at the local historical society show what a softer, sweeter, altogether different inner harbor it was before the powers-that-were began to improve it with boulders and tar. Having seen that map and those photos, I am glad I was not around to see Shirttail Point entombed in the pier.

Last year, when the pristine beaches of San Juan, Puerto Rico were filthied by an oil spill, it was presented, like all such spills, as a great crime. What is the pier but a slab of similar stuff congealed upon the delicate sand of the inner harbor? Is it less a crime because we voted to inflict it on ourselves? Accustomed to the pier though I am, it doesn't take much imagination to develop a little retroactive outrage overt the juxtaposition of the black goo that makes tarring and feathering such a gruesome punishment with the sand, the gentle waters, the shellfish.

How could this have happened? When someone came up with the idea of paving five acres of the harbor to make a pier, where were the ardent defenders of Shirttail Point? No doubt a case was made for practical uses of the proposed pier, the need for a deeper channel for fish boats, the need for increased pleasure boating capacity; no doubt it was pitched as progress. But Shirttail Point had co-existed with the 19th century heyday of Wellfleet's fishery. As for pleasure boats, how about more moorings and fewer finger piers? Accounts in newspapers of the '50s of the indictment of one local wheeler-dealer for using byproduct of the project as fill to create land for his development elsewhere in town suggest that for some, anyway, the motivation was not entirely idealistic.

Now that I have come at length to play the Monday morning quarterback, I wish more citizens of the time had stood up for Shirttail Point. I wish those in charge at the moment of the future of the town—citizens, town officers—had thought longer, harder, more soulfully. I wish that whatever opposition there was had been more effective.

If someone were today to suggest paving adjacent Mayo Beach, for whatever reason—easier rolling for the pickups of shellfishermen, well-deserved income for those in the paving trades, relief for sand-phobic beachgoers—wouldn't there be a great outcry? Wouldn't we vote it down resoundingly in town meeting? Tell me we would.

There is a book of photos called *The Place No One Knew: Glen Canyon of the Colorado*. It documents how this deep canyon upstream from the famous Grand Canyon had looked for eons before being dammed and turned into a source of hydroelectric power and a recreational lake for powerboats. The point of the title is that not enough people knew this beautiful but inaccessible canyon to save it. I felt something of the same sort of melancholy about our lost harbor. Shirttail Point: a place lots of people knew, but no enough cared enough to save.

WILD EAST

I SUPPOSE I SHOULD BLUSH to admit it, but I used to throw beer cans out of car windows.

I can remember the days when that now taboo behavior felt OK—not in my suburban New York home turf, but as part of the big adventure of crossing the desert West, with the water bag slung across the grill to cool the radiator, wet towels around our shirtless shoulders, the well-stocked cooler. The Wide Open Spaces seemed, in those days before Rachel Carson Consciousness set in, wilderness enough to stand up to the occasional beer can. Surely in such emptiness the can would return to dust before anyone else came upon it to be offended.

Is wilderness really wilderness when you have to worry about it as much as we do now, when you can threaten it with a crumpled beer can or the portable stereo turned up a few notches around the campfire for an electronic howl at the moon? Tossing a beer can was what the Wild West was all about, at least to a well-behaved boy from the eastern suburbs—more celebration than desecration.

Wellfleet has always had a funky, unregulated quality to it. Our dress code favors paint splatters and denim frayed and faded the old-fashioned way. Our building inspectors have a reputation for being no stricter than they have to be. A lot of our roads go without the civilizing benefits of pavement. We didn't even have a police force until 1948.

If some of our yards contain old cars, tools, building materials—the clutter of active, working families—well, that is just part of our identity as a real, full-bodied town, not just an antiseptic bedroom suburb or retirement destination. To some of us, anyway, this Appalachian flavor is one of the town's charms, like the boating debris left bleaching and rotting and rusting in the margins of the harbor.

In this way, Wellfleet is thematically related to the old myths of the American frontier and the Wild West, back before the farmers and politicians moved in and spoiled everything with civilization. (Some Wellfleetians, having heard the sound of the neighbor's backhoe, have moved on to the further frontier of Maine.)

This sense of ourselves as the Wild East received its first check decades ago with the advent of the National Seashore Park. The feds came in and took three-fifths of the town out of play and most locals didn't like it. The coming of the park involved a contradiction, though: It was regulation in the interest of freedom—from development. If we still retain a lot of our rural, unregulated look and feel, that is largely due to the National Seashore. The process of people just pursuing happiness and profits in the good old American free-market way has turned many a pretty, liveable little town into its opposite.

We feel nostalgia for our town when it was so rural, so wild, so underdeveloped that it didn't need regulation, when you could pitch a tent on the beach (or a beer can out of the car window). But without the restraints imposed by the Seashore there is little doubt the traditional town with its traditional freedom-loving ways would have exploited itself out of existence long before now.

Now we have another major phase of restraint, the Local Comprehensive Plan voted in at the recent town meeting to help regulate the part of town not already regulated by the park. No doubt the plan, so neatly packaged, so articulate, so . . . comprehensive, clashes with our traditional, laid-back, muddle-through style. But, as with the Seashore, this is discipline and self-consciousness in the interest of preserving what's left of the funky, underdeveloped town from itself. Such a plan is quite novel in this country, in which so much has been thoughtlessly paved, malled, exploited, trashed and generally mis-developed. We should congratulate ourselves on our passage into the era of self-restraint.

I wish my 8-year-old son could have the experience of guiltlessly and exuberantly tossing a beer can out the window when he reaches the age. But I'll settle for his having some semblance of the Wild West—or East—left for other adventures.

PLASTIC DONUT, SOULFUL PIZZA

THIS PAPER'S RECENT EDITORIAL on the resistance of Cape towns to national chains by its own admission doesn't get it. "It's hard to understand how keeping Dunkin' Donuts out is in the interest of the community at large in either Eastham or Orleans." What's all the fuss over a useful business that has been operating in other towns "apparently without creating problems"? For that matter, "Would it be such a terrible thing to offer Woods Hole residents and visitors McDonald's meals?"

So what is all the fuss about? What's wrong with chains and franchises? Why are our citizens picking on these mainstays of the American Way of Life? Well, there's the matter of the effect the proliferation of fast food joints has had on the national health; but the reason for local resistance to the big chains seems to have less to do with elevated cholesterol levels than with values. As a nation we have joked for decades about the "plastic" quality of these places, even as we have succumbed to the convenience and the clamor from the TV-saturated back seat set. By plastic we mean uniform, bland, lacking in personality. Fake.

The whole logic of a chain—the reason people who want it want it— is the mass-produced predictability, assembly-line service, programmed friendliness (even if local hirelings are the ones programmed), the feeling of connection to all the other identical places across the country and featured on everyone's TV set. As such they are a contradiction of the character and values of our towns—of localness itself. Even when, to co-opt resistance in Woods Hole, McDonalds offers to modify their façade to blend in with the local look—miniaturize the arches, nail up a few clapboards—it doesn't fool anyone. The meaning is the same: just more fakery.

It doesn't make us any friendlier to them knowing that the business is run to make profits that end up elsewhere, that with a non-local support system they have an advantage over local businesses run by our friends and neighbors, that even the construction and decoration is packaged elsewhere, bypassing local tradesmen and suppliers.

Tacitly acknowledging that they have an image problem that goes a lot deeper than image, restaurant chains have spent millions on TV ad campaigns foisting an image of themselves as jes' folks—the multi-billion-dollar corporation as the kid next door or sleepy-eyed good old boys bumbling their way to work.

Dunkin' Donuts stores have been opened in Chatham, Dennis, Harwich and Yarmouth, "apparently without creating problems," argues the editorial. But to suggest that the character of the towns in question have not been affected is naïve. Dunkin' Donuts, McDonalds, Burger King, Taco Bell, KFC and its spinoffs (notice how it finessed the no-no word "fried" out of the name?), Roy Rogers, Arbys, Pizza Hut and others that preside over the decline and fall of pizza, etc.etc.—some combination of the usual suspects constitutes whole new towns-without-souls in malls and clustered around interstate exits throughout the land. Apparently without problems: Life hasn't come to an end, people haven't died of aesthetic shock, it probably can't even be conclusively proved that the national cholesterol level has gone up. But is it so hard to understand why there would be pockets of resistance to being turned into a cliché?

ω ω ω

If it seems that Dunkin Donuts will manage to finagle its way into Orleans and Eastham despite widespread opposition, here in Wellfleet we can't seem to keep a local pizza joint despite widespread support for it.

At a special town meeting in June, the owner of Upper Crust Pizza, displaced (apparently by a lease dispute) from its traditional location, failed by a small margin to get the required two-thirds vote needed to loosen Wellfleet's zoning bylaw cap on downtown restaurants so that he could operate at a new location. Virtually everyone who spoke at the meeting declared the restaurant to be an asset to the town. But some voters were worried the zoning change would open the door to Dunkin' Donuts or McDonalds.

Providing a no-frills, thin-crust pizza at a price sensitive to locals' pocketbooks and a funky, raw atmosphere just right for this unpretentious town, Upper Crust often functioned as a community hangout, a bit of a party if you happened along at the right moment, just the thing on a blustery autumn evening. The Local Comprehensive Plan we just passed at the regular town meeting in April seems to have exactly this sort of local business in mind when, under a section titled "Strategies to Maintain Community Character," it commits the town to "support the expansion of existing business—and the establishment of new businesses—that provide goods and services for year-round residents and consider zoning changes which more effectively promote the type of economic growth and renewal that we envision."

There are businesses that must be fought in order to maintain our town's character. But when we turned down Upper Crust we lost a piece of that character.

In a prominent moment in the town meeting debate, a well-known local developer predicted in that regretful-but-realistic way developers have that, even with the defeat of the zoning change under discussion out of fear that such a change would make it easier for a chain to locate in town, it was only a matter of time before the likes of Dunkin' Donuts made Wellfleet its latest conquest. Apparently there is nothing in our current zoning that specifically discourages what would, given this town's feelings about the matter, amount to a hostile takeover of a traditional restaurant location by a national chain.

I ran it by the building inspector, our zoning enforcement officer: Why don't we have zoning that explicitly prohibits national chain restaurants as inimical to the soul of the town? He answered: Oh, I don't think you could do that. Wouldn't it be discriminatory? (Hmmm. Is that true? When it comes to redlining the law makes no distinction between minorities and multibillion-dollar burger chains?)

Isn't discrimination what our newly ratified Local Comprehensive Plan is all about, discriminating among possible scenarios of the future? It is now our official policy, if it is not Orleans', to discriminate against a future with chains and malls. Why not follow up with zoning expressing our preference for the indigenous, the funky, the real thing—home cookin'?

Is it really unconstitutional for a town to choose a future for itself?

THE DILEMMA
OF A PERFECT DAY
AT THE OCEAN

WE CAPE RESIDENTS can get pretty blasé about our ocean, especially in summer, when its effects are so unspectacular and the parking lots so crammed. But the Big Surf of August '95, spun off the quixotic hurricane Felix, commanded attention from the most jaded.

I woke one perfectly still morning hearing the muted but unmistakable roar of the surf from a mile and a half away, punctuated, believe it or not, by the crack of the occasional individual breaker. Such a sound, and the knowledge of its carrying so far, generates excitement in storm season. But in the dog days of August, when the surf often amounts to more than a ripple turning over with a gentle slap and lazy hiss? What was going on over there?

Obeying the summons, in 10 minutes I was standing at the top of the cliff of sand, the whole ocean spread out before me. Under a brilliant sky the gleaming curls were huge and long, heaving themselves up out of a calm sea, up and up and—ahhh—over, with that crack I had heard while lying in bed. Really more of a crunch, when you listened closely; or whoomph—choose your own personal favorite approximation of that perfectly satisfying, utter, explosive collapse.

I was not alone at the early morning vigil. The front row of parking spaces, where ordinarily you might find one domestic refugee in a pickup sipping tepid coffee and reading the paper, was filled with ocean groupies. Many of my fellow gawkers were surfers, checking the waves with expert eyes, their cognoscenti's respect anchoring our collective excitement. Surfing felt like the right thing to do—get out there and play with those boisterous waves, engage the medium, meet the ocean on its own terms. But what about us mere mortals without the skill with board and body? Beyond our rapt voyeurism, our hapless wows and whoas, how should we rise to this occasion?

There is the meditative approach: just stand there, breathe deeply, and try to take it all in. But that seemed too passive. One wanted to respond. Bounce down the cliff, race to the water's edge, get upclose and personal with this galumphing ocean. Imitate the dogs, make little runs at the foam, play a bit of tag with flicks of mama ocean's tail. A bicycler, seduced from his exercise routine, had toted his bike down the cliff and was wobbling along the ragged interface of sand and surf, until he began to think about the effect of the salt water on his machine.

By midmorning vacationing beachgoers would be flipping frisbees and spiking volleyballs with a special keenness on this energized stage. Some would offer themselves up to be battered and rolled by the crumbles of waves that break 200 feet beyond where any but the surfers dare to go.

But what should I do with these frolicsome waves? Write about it? Nahhh. Those waves were so huge and so perfectly formed you can't, as they say, capture them in words. Rather, I felt as though the brilliance of the scene had captured me. Kerouac sat by the Pacific and tried to record its voice: "ka bloom, kerplosh, ah ropey otter barnacled be, crowsh . . ." (*Big Sur*). Writer and ocean both come out sounding like a jerk.

Finally, there was nothing to do but turn my back, trudge up the steep cliff through heavy sand. After work, maybe, get some people together, build a bonfire in salute. Maybe even stay on and fall asleep rolled in a blanket, perchance to catch some of the sound of that surf in one's dreams.

WILL IT PLAY IN PEORIA?

WITH 60,000 WATTS, six times its former power, radio station WOMR (92.1 FM), "outermost radio" as it calls itself, is no longer the marginal, edge-city phenomenon we have known and loved. At least not in its reach. It has bitten off a sizable chunk of the Real World, as the land beyond the Eastham-Orleans rotary can feel to denizens of the Outer Cape.

The newly muscular WOMR is like a chain store in reverse. If every fast-food chain and cell phone company in the land is intent on shoe-horning its way onto the Outer Cape, WOMR is now empowered to unleash its—our—indigenous culture on an unsuspecting world.

There is a paradox here. While WOMR has gone regional in its reach, its product has always been insistently local. You could say its product is localness. Unlike most public radio (WGBH for instance), WOMR is a true community station with an amateur feel to it (in the root sense of doing it for love rather than money). Virtually all its DJs are volunteers from the immediate area. The guy in the checkout line at the grocery, the woman walking her dog down your road—these are the media stars of our radio station. The personality of the station is created by a range of real voices, by on-air pauses, mistakes, giggles about mistakes, the texture of the moment.

To a large extent the station has always seemed like friends and neighbors broadcasting to each other. Sometimes in the depth of winter you get the feeling that it is just you and your DJ friend, maybe a half-dozen waitresses at the restaurant, nail bangers at a few scattered job sites listening in. Given the coziness, it's easy to be interactive, get on the phone and make a song request, report the temperature or snow depth in your neck of the woods.

The interesting question is: What will others in WOMR's newly expanded radioland make of this local color and texture? Eric Williams' jolly nastiness, often at the expense of suburban mores, Chuck Cole's keep-the-faith updated '60s, Magic's magic, Parker's Planets, Scott Penn's breathy romance, the kid voices, the vulnerable aging voices, strident voices, the grouchy voices—how will they sound to the Real World? WOMR's emphasis on gay culture and progressive politics in general is perfectly appropriate for the Outer Cape market, which on many occasions has gone 99 percent for Representative Studds. But how will it be received by an audience that supports Rush Limbaugh? How will WOMR play in Peoria? (Metaphorically, I guess this is Peoria.)

More important, what becomes of the local when it is exported? How about a feedback effect? Won't DJs, aware of a different audience with a higher percent of Them than Us, begin to change their style and substance, as most of us do depending on whom we are talking to? Won't Eric begin to pull punches knowing that his audience now includes some of the tourists he loves to satirize? Will Chuck go on broadcasting his grandfather's poetry or the worldwide surfing report knowing that WOMR now reaches where, sadly enough, 40-year-olds don't surf and the prevailing view is that grandparents should be neither seen nor heard?

Won't the station begin to feel it ought to clean up its act, tidy up the voices, remove the grumbles, the umms, the throat-clearings, all that good texture that bespeaks broadcasters comfortable with the audience and in turn endears the station to its local listeners? Won't the station feel it ought (or the FCC require it) to start reflecting the more conservative politics of its new audience by giving equal time to some gay-bashing, feminist-baiting listener of the Rush Limbaugh stripe?

WOMR: Congratulations, guys, on the upgrade. If you got it, flaunt it. But remember what "it" is. This is a great chance to preach to the unconverted (not that preaching is your style). Stay loose, local and progressive. Don't be distracted by your new audience.

STRETCHING
THE SEASON

ONE OF THE MOST POIGNANT markers of the end of summer is the last swim of the season. We may be surrounded by water, but we are merely tourists in that medium, compared with the fulltime denizens. It is hard to imagine calling that icy, desolate world home in the three seasons when we retreat to our dry, heated spaces. Probably the way a lot of our tourists view the thought of spending winter on the Outer Cape.

We are told that water in some steamy, swampy tropical version was our ancient element, the womb from which our prototypes crawled—for what reason I can't imagine. Immersion in the warmed water of summer is a sort of reconnection with those beginnings. But around this time of year that atavistic comfort and soul nourishment is lost to us for the next eight months. (The Polar Bear Club's ritual swim on New Year's Day is, of course, not an exception. It is a celebration of our organism's powers of resistance, a macho—or masochistic—plunge, with shuddering and sputtering and noisy good cheer, into an alien environment.)

For some time now I have been wondering when that last swim would be. I swam at the end of a jog on October 13th. The water at my local pond was tolerable, but admittedly most of the pleasure was in the basking afterward on a bit of dock conveniently deserted by its summer people. That and in certain moral points one gives oneself for copping a swim so late in the season.

A week and a couple of blustery autumn fronts later, air temperature reaching for 70, I walked over to the pond with a swim in mind, but ended up thinking better of it after standing thigh deep for some minutes. The water temperature was not crucially lower than the previous time, but the air was a few degrees cooler and there was just too much breeze. My spirit just refused to rise to the occasion and I settled for a disgruntled nap on the dock.

Summer swimming is an easy habit here in the pond district of Wellfleet, almost an addiction. We are in and out of one pond or another all day, running down for dips before breakfast, at noon, before dinner, even at dusk. But as much as I want to think of September as the summer month, by halfway through, as air temperatures dip into the 70s and water temperatures into the 60s (from a summer high of mid-70s or higher), going for a swim begins to seem less an indulgence and more of an adventure. I begin giving myself moral credit for each swim. And to wonder which swim will be the last.

Surely by the time this column appears, the last day of October, Thanksgiving barely three weeks off, that last swim will be history, and known to be such: Oh yeah, I'll realize—that swim on Friday the 13th turned out to be the last swim of the summer. But it hasn't turned out yet. It isn't getting any warmer, and I don't plan to get any braver about cold water. But I'm still entertaining the possibility of yet one more ritual immersion. For one thing, there was last fall's prolonged mellowness, a friend's message on the answering machine on an unnaturally warm day at least a week into November that he was heading for a last swim in the pond, wouldn't we like to join him? (I was secretly glad I didn't get the message until too late to do anything about it, but I got considerable vicarious pleasure from his November swim.)

I knew a guy who had the thought that if you keep swimming every day, since the temperature drop is never very great from one day to the next, you should never come to the day when suddenly you can't get in. Theoretically you could get through the winter that way. Seems to me he got beyond Thanksgiving testing his theory and then I lost track of him.

It is occurring to me that there is an analogy here with aging and the tendency toward death. Some denial of those realities in this resistance to the dying of the year. If you just keep running, keep on doing whatever it is you do day after day, why will there ever come a day when you don't do it? Just keep on truckin', keep on keepin' on. Just keep on living and you'll never die.

There's got to be a flaw in this line of thinking somewhere, but I find it comforting.

DEVELOPMENT BLUES

BILLY NEWCOMB USED TO ROAM this neck of the Wellfleet woods. (That should be Mr. Newcomb to me, I suppose, washashore that I am, but Billy is how I have always heard him referred to). Billy was a descendant of the Wellfleet oysterman made famous by Thoreau's account of his visit to him. A couple of times he came to inspect progress on our cottage while we were building it in the early '80s. He died sometime back. I assume he still haunts the neighborhood, although he may be quitting in disgust soon.

We're singin' the development blues these days. We recently became aware that the 16 acres in back of us, one of the last large chunks of undeveloped land in town, are to be transformed into building lots. Surveyors have been tromping through the woods leaving them decorated with those festive pink plastic ribbons. I have seen the plan dividing the 16 acres of forest into the maximum number of lots allowed by Wellfleet's three-quarter acre zoning—20.

I have calculated that the 20-foot wide roads shown on the plan and required by the town to access a subdivision of this size will cover more than an acre of the 16 with pavement. An acre of pavement. Another acre will be taken up by the required 10-foot strip of artificially landscaped embankments on either side of the roads.

Oh yeah, gonna have us a suburb in our backyard.

The worst sort of euphemism, the word "development." A positive word when used to allude to a child's growing powers or turning an idea into a painting or a novel. But when we hear the word development used in a real estate connection, a lot of us want to run the other way. I wish we could. We are mourning in advance the loss of these woods, which we always knew were someone's property but felt like just woods. They sat there, unforgiveably undeveloped for woods caught outside the National Seashore corral, the sun shining on them, rain, snow and wind having their way with them by turns. To tell the truth, I couldn't say what went on back there in the way of hawks nesting, red foxes romping, raccoons dividing up the booty from raids on our garbage cans. What went on was less important to us than what did not. The real treasure was simple fallowness, the lack of development.

This is a neighborhood of sand roads. A mere one lane in width, they can be inconvenient for cars, as when one must back up to a widening to let another pass. But they are soft, sinuous, undulating—easy on the eyes, easy on the legs. They slow the few cars down, making us feel more comfortable letting our kids play near the roads or ride their bikes on them. One of these roads, the Old King's Highway, was for hundreds of years the Route 6 of its era. The "old" in the name of another of these sand roads reminds us that it was the traditional way to get to the local pond, predating the paved road from town.

In fact, there was an "ancient way," as they are charmingly referred to in official documents, running off one corner of our land and back through the 16 acres. I've seen it on old maps. Though barely driveable when we built here 14 years ago, it was a connection to the ancient ways of the people who lived here before us. My son and I would go out once in a while and do a little pruning to keep it alive as a path, an act that seemed less trespassing than caretaking.

The development, with its 40-foot swaths of paved roadway, will obliterate 16 acres of Wellfleet history. These paved roads will be much more convenient, respectable roads. They feel like a cancer on our neighborhood and the quality of our lives.

I know, we are a classic case of "I've got mine." Maybe Billy Newcomb felt the same way when we started to build—there goes the neighborhood. And we know how the Native Americans felt about Billy's ancestors. Things change.

The previous owner of the land, a neighbor, was perfectly within his rights spelled out in the zoning bylaws voted in years ago by we the people. No doubt in griping I am violating a point of etiquette that says you don't complain when a neighbor pursues happiness by disposing of his own land in a perfectly legal manner. Guy's gotta do what a guy's gotta do. And yet . . . how can we who love this place the way it is do less than bear witness that there is something of value that is being lost here, forever. And that as an act of buying and selling and zoning-as-usual, it could have been different.

Arriving after the change, my future neighbors in this Levittown-in-the-woods won't know the difference. We will.

GETTING REAL

IT'S TOWN MEETING TIME again. Almost certainly
Wellfleet's attempts to shape a future will themselves be
shaped by a depressingly predictable conflict: pro-
development vs. anti-development. Pro-business vs. anti-
business. Growth vs. conservation. Sociologically put:
working people with families needing more opportunity
vs. empty nesters passionate about preserving the town
they chose to retire in.

We seem stuck in this rigid dichotomy. And yet I
assume most of us would resist simplistic pigeonholing on
either side of the growth issue. Carpenters, waitresses,
house cleaners, storekeepers, fishermen—even, possibly,
developers—do not regard themselves as last among
admirers of our town. In fact, they have often deliberately
made a decision, against economic self-interest, to live in
a place like this for much the same reason as retired
people—the charm and quality-of-life of this relatively
undeveloped town.

And it seems just as true that when our retired or
semi-retired "anti-growth" citizens talk about loving this
town they are not talking about nice old houses and
scenery alone. There is something about the ongoing life
of the town, the variety of characters one is likely to
encounter at the library or hanging out at the local

restaurant, the sense of a community that keeps humming, to ears attuned to the sound, all winter long, that constitutes a considerable part of our charm.

I imagine few of us of either faction, when looking at one of those old photos of Main Street of a few decades ago lined with Newcomb's Soda Shop, millinery and sundries stores, the Wellfleet Hotel and other features of smalltown life compare the present lineup favorably. No one is glad the candy store burned down 20 years ago and has not been replaced, that there has not been a laundry in town for many years. I don't think we actually prefer to have to do our serious grocery shopping in Orleans. People from both sides of the growth issue deplored the post office moving to Route 6 and removing one of the traditional bulwarks of our downtown.

In fact, it seems to me that a lot of people in this town share a vision of a diversified, fully functioning Real Town, a vision that ought to be able to help us transcend the pro-growth, anti-growth rut we are in. A focus on Real Town as a guiding concept would make clear certain guidelines in the way we think about development. Neither a kneejerk anti-business stance nor a kneejerk pro-business stance is consistent with the goal of have a Real Town.

No development should be permitted on the basis of profits or salaries alone. National chain stores should be opposed by all as entirely inconsistent with our character and values. But there should be more flexibility with regard to proposed new business, with less emphasis on quotas and more emphasis on appropriateness. We hear this term "appropriate development" thrown around a lot. Just what might constitute appropriate development for a town such as this?

How about an affordable, funky, year-round second-run movie house in the central district (with popcorn with real butter)? A local grocery store with selection and prices that would make feasible cutting down on those shopping trips to Orleans? How about rebirth of the laundromat?

An off-season writers' conference or film festival that would exploit and enhance our reputation as a haven for artists and writers (why should Cannes and Breadloaf get all the action?). How about some outdoor cafes and markets with colorful awnings and umbrellas and live music to enliven the wasteland of our misbegotten pier?

I don't think anybody wants to see Wellfleet slowly become a Cape version of Sturbridge or a narrowland suburb, a gallery town or retirement community. Rather, a Real Town of a certain sort.

STRUTTIN' OUR STUFF

WATCHING THE FOURTH of July Parade with family from other parts, I felt proud of us. Now this was a Wellfleet parade.

Seems like the parade had been in a bit of a decline. The last couple of years it had been mostly blaring, raspy fire engine horns and solemn dignitaries—hardly our town self-image. Not a rhythm section in the whole thing.

I remember my wife and I saying to each other that next year our neighborhood ought to do a float. Better to be in a boring parade than have to watch one. A lot of others must have been feeling something of the same thing, because this one was a return to the exuberance and wackiness of old. The Raspberry Berets, Lisa on a truck wailing on bongos and congas while exercising with her whistle tight discipline over her struttin' ladies' Kazoo Korp. Two perfectly voluptuous ladies dressed in the classic Spanish manner to the rose clenched in their teeth riding two voluptuous horses for a local restaurant. A children's steel band followed, in a reverse Pied Piper, by certain parents gyrating in the thrall of those spicy Caribbean dance rhythms (as well as in the exhaust fumes of the truck).

There were the usual official town office floats, the police, the fire engines. The selectmen float is always reassuring—if they dare to show their faces in this public way, how bad can things be? One aggrieved citizen greeted them with his second annual stationary float (a moored float?) from his yard on the parade route, a toilet and sign: CONTRIBUTIONS FOR SELECTMEN EDUCATION FUND.

It was Wellfleet putting its parts on parade. There were neighborhood floats, occupation floats, the wonderful library float leafletting the audience with little books, gender politics floats.

It was Wellfleet struttin' its stuff, the town digging itself. There was less performer/observer distance than is usual with such things. Enthusiastic appreciation went both ways, those on the floats merrily pelting bystanders with everything from candy and nuts to blueberry muffinettes. Those along the parade route laughing, shouting at their kids, friends and neighbors on the floats.

Hey, look, there's so and so . . . Isn't that Sally? Hey, you're looking good. Hey, throw some candy our way. Where's Ben? Oh, there he is…Hey Ben. Oh, he doesn't see us, he's concentrating so hard on that drum.

Suddenly you would see a small family with stroller and dog on a leash who struck you a certain way or maybe someone on a bike cruising the scene with a little bit of style and start clapping for them as just another float. All right, lookin' good. Or making your way down Main Street to find some friends to sit with you would, in the spirit of things, start to feel like a float yourself. Hey, we're a float. Why not? I thought about making up a sign: WE ARE A FLOAT or FLOATING IS A STATE OF MIND Or how about (since we were proceeding up the down parade route): STILL FLOATING UPSTREAM (after all these years). Or: STILL AFLOAT. Hey, why not? Life is a parade, everyone's a float—or afloat, one hopes.

Good stuff, this parade. A most un-American sort of parade despite the plethora of flags—not a McDonalds or Disney float anywhere to be seen. A most un-American sort of parade in that typical, indispensable American Way: short on speeches about freedom, long on freedom.

PUSHING THE RIVER

AN OLD FRIEND FROM NEW YORK CITY and I were discussing our strikingly different choices of where to live. It must be very painful, she said, to live where so much is undeveloped. Undevelopment means the potential for development. Every new development must feel like a little tragedy.

One of the main features, for better or worse, of urban living is that much of the painful change has already happened. Whatever tears were shed at the lopping off of Boston's hills to fill in and tame its original charming but inefficient waterfront are long forgotten. The pristine rivers, forests, topography and early settlements of the original Manhattan are so profoundly buried under layer upon layer of pavement, pollution and poverty-scape that they are but an historical curiosity, no longer with the power to hurt.

The city may be the ultimate monument to exploitation of everything in sight, landscape, resources, people. But I knew what my friend meant: In some ways it is more painful to live here, in a relatively unexploited region. Papers are filled every day with controversial change and threatened change.

The outrage of the paid packing of the Home Depot hearing with Christmas Tree Shops workers from off-

Cape didn't exactly help the digestion of breakfast the other morning. This morning, along with the ongoing Home Depot wars, there is a letter about another Burger King trying to take root. "Old Cape Cod Goes Up For Sale," grieved a front page headline a week or two ago about the proposed subdivision of 30 acres in Truro. (This is a place where nostalgia is front page news.)

But why should it be painful, this change? Why should it feel like an assault, a barrage, a rape? Isn't change one of the most basic elements of life, just part of the flow, as natural as the seasons following one another? Maybe those of us who suffer from the daily news about what's happening to the Cape just have an attitude problem. Certainly the developers and their supporters think so. Change is inevitable, they say. The Cape is changing anyway, so let 'er rip, get out of the way, don't push the river, as we used to say back in the 'sixties. (Sounds to me like the wonderfully helpful advice to a rape victim to relax and enjoy herself).

Certainly, change is part of the fabric and process of life, but that doesn't make it less painful. Relating to it is a bit more complicated than riding the developer's magic carpet into the future, or giving into the inevitable and magically transforming your rape into Great Sex.

Change doesn't happen "anyway", independent of what people do, of what you do. You are in the middle of it, part of its process, helping to determine at what rate and how, in what direction, things will change. Things don't change impersonally, like the succession of the seasons, but personally. Things change because this fellow citizen wants to make money, this citizen does this, these neighbors get on this committee and do this . . .or that.

Things change in a way that makes developers happy in part because this or that person gets up in public and says things like "the Cape is changing anyway." A letter to the editor the other day said, objecting to my heartless ganging up on megabusiness in a recent column, that we are all equally responsible for what she admits is a mess. But those who fight the mess on committees and hearings and in letters to the editor make that sort of change less likely to happen. Those who fail to show up, or who write letters saying things like were all equally responsible for the rape of the Cape (i.e., there is no enemy, the enemy is us, so why struggle?) make it more likely to happen.

The owner of The Christmas Tree Shops claims innocence about busing workers to pack that Home Depot hearing. But surely somebody did something. It didn't happen "anyway," it happened because somebody put those workers up to it and those workers, however sheepishly some of them apparently felt afterwards when the meaning of their actions sank in, did the deed. (Don't you just love a bargain? Only 50 bucks a day for the use of a human soul.)

As we can plainly see, big companies have no problem understanding what a small minority, motivated by profits, can accomplish by enough determined pushing and shoving. They know change doesn't happen outside human agency.

Those of us motivated by love of a place, of a home, of a certain way of life—we, too, have not only the right but the obligation to stand wherever we are in the tide of things, the flow of time and history, and fight for what we care for.

WELLFLEETLAND

ONE OF THE HOTTEST architectural movements of recent years has been the master-planning of whole subdivisions or malls on the model of old-fashioned towns. Seaside, a development on the Florida panhandle, not only has the look of a traditional town with the charm of indigenous architecture; it incorporates certain patterns of living inherent in traditional towns, especially a scale which encourages walking to shops and public gathering places.

Disney's Celebration (why do I want to put that in quotes?) near Orlando, just revving up this year, is another example of the trend. As the name implies, it is a celebration of traditional American culture that one might expect to find as an exhibit in Disney World nearby, but it has jumped the fence and it's out there in the real world, an instant old-fashioned town. You could go live in it.

A recent *New York Times* article featured Rochester's Wegman's, a supermarket taken to the next level, a grocery store reconceptualized as a whole community under one roof—not just one-stop shopping but one-top living. The idea was to reconfigure the typical megastore's hangar-like atmosphere and ugly overhead lighting as individual departments, like little European markets, restaurants, a pharmacy, and so on, arranged along meandering lanes (instead of typical aisles) with more intimate lighting and indoor park benches for resting. It's one of the biggest stores ever but human scaled like a small town.

What such malls and master-planned developments have in common is a recognition that—of all things—there is something about the old-fashioned small town that still has appeal for us. That has, perhaps, universal value. In other words, having been instrumental, through the malling and suburbanizing of America, in eviscerating Main Street, these megabusiness forces turn around and reproduce it, turning fakes of it into yet more malls and suburban development.

I have a modest proposal to make. Here in Wellfleet we have a little, traditional town still largely intact. The trouble is, a lot of the original functions of the town have closed down and moved up-Cape. We limp along during the winter months with a restaurant or two, a traditional-looking market on Main Street that functions largely as a convenience store, such basics as a liquor store, pharmacy and several churches. We spend a lot of time and energy worrying about how to stimulate local business without destroying the charm of our town and its natural setting. Here's my idea: if the big time developers are going to all the trouble of reproducing the American small town in mall land, why not stop thinking of ourselves as a traditional town fallen on lean times and start thinking of ourselves as a newly designed and built mall, a Cape version of Seaside or Celebration?

We could sell ourselves to Disney since they seem so good at making the fake traditional pay off. And why wouldn't they be interested since it would save them the whole cost of having to construct us—no architect will ever design a more authentic theme park version of us than we are already. We could even use our original name, although in quotes, of course. Or Wellfleetland. A clear plastic dome over us, to get a handle on our ornery weather, might help in selling the whole idea. With the Disney genius for special effects they'll have simulated– but warm and dry—nor'easters up and running in no time.

Or better still, incorporate as a business and do it ourselves.

Wellfleetland, an idea has whose time has come. The answer to Wellfleet's underdevelopment woes. Of course, to be consistent with the Wellfleetland concept, we would have to move the Post Office back into the center of town, where it belongs. We would need to rewrite the bylaws to prohibit the suburban-style, paved cul-de-sac development that is now required, ban gawky communications towers along with megastores and malls both mini- and maxi. Afterall, they would spoil the small town atmosphere.

THE SAFE PLACE
CONCEPT

"TOWN MOURNS LOSS OF FRIEND, loss of security" read the headline for one of the stories about the murder of Linda Silva. Yes, quite clearly there is more to our shock and grief at this crime than the loss of a member of the community. What's at stake is our whole concept of our home as a secure place.

Usually I think of Provincetown, Truro, Wellfleet and, when I'm feeling charitable, Eastham as all part of the same stompin' grounds, sharing an identity as wilder, less developed, end-of-the-roadish. However, since this still unsolved killing I notice I am making a lot of the distance from my particular piece of this turf, Wellfleet, to Provincetown. Geographical distance (hey, that's 16 miles from here), conceptual distance (well, it is more urban ...). Anything to create emotional distance, make myself feel safer.

The great thing about concepts is their comforting absoluteness. In the three-plus decades since first setting foot here, I have always regarded Wellfleet as a Safe Place. Not sort of safe. Not safe compared, say, to Boston or Hyannis. No: not relatively safe but inherently, intrinsically, Absolutely Safe. A place you not only don't have to lock your door, you don't even think about it, you can't even remember if you still have the key. Where a woman skinny-dipping by herself at a secluded pond need worry only about getting busted by a Seashore ranger.

Oh, sure, there was that big mid-'70s bust of a million dollar drug boat tied up in our harbor. But that was essentially outsider crime, not really of this place. The role of the local cops was mainly just trying not to fumble the hand-off to the feds. More recently we have been the site of a search for a missing and presumed murdered girl from Maryland. Turns out Wellfleet is the kind of place serial killers might like to stash a body. Even this lurid possibility seems so unthreatening to our self-image as a Safe Place that most of us follow the search with the same interest we would the story of a whale washed up on shore or an exotic bird blown here by a hurricane.

Other assaults on security have been more ominous. About four years ago there was a murder, vaguely gang related, right in front of a class full of kids in the Dartmouth high school. Around the same time just across the canal a girl was shot while riding in a school bus. But then that was Across the Bridge, crucially part of the mainland, not Cape Cod. Conceptually, we were still safe, if a little nervous.

Not too many years ago I had all of the Cape down as a Safe Place, a refuge from an America being increasingly characterized as violent society. That made for a nice Upcape buffer zone. Of course, reading the local papers I couldn't avoid seeing that crimes—violent crimes, even the occasional murder—did in fact occur on this side of the canal. Then there was that exchange student hit in the neck by a bullet apparently fired from a bridge over the Mid-Cape Highway. Violent America is undeniably headed in this direction, along with the malls and the franchises. My concept of the Cape as a safe haven shrank to our part of it.

This unsolved murder in Provincetown, though, hits too close to home. It challenges the whole concept of Safe Place, as does the story about young Wellfleetians being involved in a rape or in fights with Napi's Brooklyn kitchen help. As do stories of drugs and knife possession in the Nauset Middle School. Let's face it, it's getting pretty hard to defend the concept of Wellfleet as an oasis in a desert of crime.

Recently, re-reading Thornton Wilder's *Our Town*, everybody's classic about small town life, I was surprised to discover that in the first decade of the 20th century people in fictional Grover's Corners, N.H. started locking their doors at night. "Ain't been any burglars in town yet," says the Stage Manager commentator, "but everybody's heard about 'em. On the whole, things don't change much around here." Actually that sounds like a pretty momentous change, going from everybody trusting the world enough to leave their houses unlocked to everybody locking them up. The threat is perceived to be from the outside, so in that sense it isn't a change in the town per se. But the belief in the minds of townsfolk that the world is no longer safe—that is a change in the town. A watershed moment in the life of a place, I'd say.

What surprised me was how long ago this locking started, almost 100 years ago—even before World War I, often cited as the start of the modern world's harsh realities, back when you would think there would be little to be afraid of. Who is right? The residents of sleepy little Grover's Corners, N.H., way back then, or us? Were they being overly cautious? Have we been so romantically in love with the idea of this being a Safe Place that it blinds us to the statistical reality? What is the reality here?

We wait for more information about this killing, hoping to find it related meaningfully, if terribly, to some domestic or communal drama and therefore not simply an example of the random violence and rampant disregard for human life we associate with elsewhere. We hope it will not be an infestation of violent America that will prove fatal to an essential element in the quality of our lives.

THE IMPLIED OCEAN

BEFORE MOVING TO WELLFLEET, I used to be shocked to hear friends who lived here full time confess they didn't visit the beach all that often. What? Really? But we drive hours for a few precious hours at the beach. How could you not be there all the time?

Having grown up landlocked, I found the idea of living near or on a large body of water indescribably exciting. Moving here seemed like a fulfillment of an impossible dream: all the ocean I wanted. Like a starving man at a buffet, I didn't think I could ever get enough. I'm sure I will never be able to convey this to my son, who has grown up here.

When and if I move here, I would tell my blasé local friends, I'll start every day communing with the ocean and end it with sunset at a bay beach.

But now that I have lived here for a few years I find myself falling into the same slacker behavior. Especially in winter, of course. Weeks go by between trips to the back side, all of a mile and a half away. And what visits there are often take the form of jumping in the car and running over to check on it: yep, still there; jump back in the car, zip home.

One of my jogs takes me down Ocean View Drive for a stretch, but that doesn't count as a trip to the beach. In fact, that I would run down that road for a mile hearing and glimpsing the surf through low cuts in the dunes, and not be lured to its edge, is further proof of my apostasy.

On the other hand, I have found that without all the pressure of getting the most out of your two days or two weeks of vacation, of extracting every last bit of whatever it is you can get from a face-to-face with the sea, you find yourself tuning into what could be called the implied ocean. There is the sense of our seabound situation not just over at the beach but all around, the smell and feel of it in the air. There is the circumstantial evidence of the gulls cruising endlessly overhead. There is the roar of surf, quite distinct, even to the crack of individual breakers, coming that mile and a half over the pines during many nights in the winter when it is very still or the wind is in the east.

There is the Cape light made so famous by Joel Meyerowitz's book of photographs. At sundown, pink, fluffy clouds carry rumors of sunset over the harbor. (We used to run over in the car with glasses of wine a couple of times a week; now it's more like twice a year.)

There is the ubiquitous sand coming up every time you scratch our thin topsoil, not to mention all the beach that gets tracked into the house and the mini-dune you have to pour out of your shoes half the time when you go to put them on. The Outer Cape is all beach, a sandbar with a scraggly forest barely hanging on. We are always at the beach.

There are so many smells that bring the sea to us back here in the woods, perhaps even more sharply than if we were at water's edge, where we might be distracted from the smells by the sights or by our expectations of a time at the beach: You walk out the door and are swimming in fresh, raw, salt air, or the smell that comes with low clouds or fog. You certainly don't need to check the chart or drive over to find out when low tide is.

There are days in winter when the wind is rising in the trees and the day is completely transformed by an approaching nor'easter. Your body, as you go about your day, is electrified by the rumored storm. And, more than likely, unlike the first couple of winters, you won't drive over to check the storm surf. You know now that if it's a big storm blowing 50-60 knots you won't want to get the car anywhere near the edge of the dune if you value your paint job or the transparency of your windshield. You know that you won't be able to look at the surf anyway for fear of getting your eyes full of stinging, airborne beach. You know now, as did the pre-tourism settlers on the Outer Cape who would never build a house perched up for the ocean view, that an implied nor'easter is about all a person can take in.

Sometimes I worry that the inconceivable has happened, that the sea has become mere background as the tourist romance has been replaced by real life; that I am taking the ocean for granted. But I really think that I have just learned, like others, that our watery situation permeates all of our life. We are truly saturated with it. The implied ocean makes all the difference to living here.

BRAVE STAND

WELLFLEET'S BRAVE STAND against the telecommunications industry appears to be over. It wasn't quite another Wounded Knee, but there were some of the same feelings.

In several high-spirited, well attended hearings during '95 and '96 we turned down in no uncertain terms two proposed 190-foot communications towers. The first one was to go between some backyards and the Seashore boundary, the second with its feet planted at the edge of our cherished wetland of Duck Creek. The company's lawyer seemed genuinely surprised, perhaps his feelings a little hurt, at the ferocity of our reaction. Read our lips, we said: No communications towers here. No communications tower anywhere in this town.

We were scathing in our rejection of this proposed boost to our admittedly down-in-the-heel standard of living. Let others pant after electronic ubiquity. We don't want beepers and phones echoing around our secluded ponds as visitors check their stocks from pondside. Furthermore, we don't want to have to worry about the health consequences of those microwaves being beamed into our houses and schools. (At our hearings scientific studies were read into evidence; quite clearly there are, while nothing conclusive either way, concerns.)

We spoke passionately about the inappropriateness to our horizontal skyline of gangly vertical structures. One had the feeling that even an offer to relocate the Eiffel Tower here would have been turned down.

When the lawyers, dropping the sensitivity act, hinted darkly that we wouldn't get away with this shabby treatment of what amounted to a public utility, that things were afoot at the state and federal level, that we'd see. . . we replied: Go ahead, make our day.

It was exhilarating, our rejection of the telecommunications industry's ambitions for our standard of living. A bit of David and Goliath. In our innocence we thought: we have carried the day, the people have spoken and that's that. Democracy in action. America at its best.

But then came the news that, as the company lawyers had threatened, the recently enacted Federal Telecommunications Act had decreed that no town has the right to opt out of the grid, even if every last person in that town votes against it. Our Planning Board, having read the fine print of the new law (as well as the writing on the wall), came up with a bylaw spelling out ways of getting the industry into our town in the most painless way possible. And there we were at Town Meeting in the fall passing the bylaw, since we had been told there was no alternative, 168-3. If you didn't know the background to that vote, you would think we had suddenly done an aboutface and were welcoming those towers with open arms. If you did know about the strong opposition, it was kind of ironic, kind of sad.

Where do you get off, the industry, and the feds echoing them, said in essence, thinking a little town like you can resist what passes in the Great World for a higher standard of living? I guess we get off here.

EXORCISING
URBAN GHOSTS

I JUST RETURNED from a work trip to our old house in Hartford, that troubled city that still darkens the edge of our lives.

Five years ago we made the move from our neighborhood of old, boxy houses darkened by looming maples to a new house on an acre of Wellfleet woods under the big Cape sky. We traded the constraints of city traffic and deadbolt locks that had to be locked for the shortest trip out, for a key-free and almost traffic light-free existence; Hartford's urban problems for the Outer Cape's solution.

Of course, none of us who wash ashore here on the Outer Cape get away clean. Urban/suburban reality is thrown up at us in the newspapers and TV news. It pursues us across the canal in the form of disturbing stories about crime and suburban teen problems in up-Cape cities. It plagues us like a recurring nightmare. It is the underbelly of all of our lives.

None of us get away clean, but we didn't get away at all, really. While most make a complete financial break and sell their house, we found it necessary to keep ours for rental income to support our Cape habit. Our lives are still partly back there, one foot still mired in the urban quagmire. We have an investment—when you look closely, a building with people in it—to care for.

Hartford is, according to newspaper stories: a decaying infrastructure, a school system so incompetent the state had to take it over, and driveby shootings—daylight shootings, driveby shootings, crossfire killings. And I own a piece of it. My crumbling house is a little piece of this crumbling city.   If our collective urban past is, metaphorically speaking, a dark cellar to the Outer Cape's cheery upstairs room-with-a-view, I have an actual, unmetaphorical basement to contend with.

And I find it is that 100 year-plus basement that has come to embody my troubled urban connection: its flaking stone foundation, crumbling mortar, frayed, asbestos-wrapped pipes, cobwebs from the Depression, a dank smell that oppresses my heart every time I start down those squeaking old stairs.

When I first took over the house from the estate of a woman who had owned it since the early '30s, much of the time running it as a boarding house, the basement was ankle deep in slimy decades-old magazines, moldy clothing and excrement from a backed-up sewer line. I called Roto Rooter and cleansed the Augean stable, saving all the interesting relics; and then started adding my own layers of life's detritus, including inches of saw dust from my table saw, old house parts, as I renovated the upstairs, stacks of old wood, boxes of clothing and books, all of which became forever endowed and most rendered unusable with malodorous essence of old basement.

It had been years since I really looked at that basement. The floor was filthy, like a river bottom, from recent and not-so-recent floods. The place seemed terminally uncared for, a place people—including me in my infrequent visits—walked through as quickly as possible, eyes straight ahead on way to the washing machine (incongruous exile from the upper world). It seemed to symbolize all that I wish I could put behind me, the chaotic, obscene, dark, foul, deeply incompetent in my life's situation. I despaired.

But then, because I really have no choice, I began once again to clean that basement, lugging out to the curb the mildewed leavings of recent tenants, large plastic bags of unspeakables, including a piece of stained, corrugated cardboard plastered to the floor from under which had scurried a small, moist lizard of some sort. (All this to be relocated by city servants to some other urban sacrificial space; but hey, out of sight, out of mind.)

How I had resisted leaving the Cape on a nice spring weekend to confront my urban roots. But with every musty item carted lightward it felt more like the right thing to be doing, purging this city basement. At some point I even began joking about moving back to Hartford and taking up residence in the basement as a way of exorcising the ghosts in that dark corner of my economic and emotional life. It was just a joke—we have never felt the slightest inclination to return to the city—but I began to feel how it might be satisfying to move there, to take possession of this foulest corner of our lives and, because we would have to, make it liveable. Really scour the place, finally expunge every last relic, the baggage of the years, burn it in a ritual pyre if the city would allow it; vacuum the floor, the walls, the joists, the ancient knob-and-tube wiring, wrap up those asbestos pipes. And finally, fill a big brush with thick, white paint, smush it into every crevice. Slowly, by our living there and working on it, redeem this space.

No doubt the tenants upstairs would begin to think of me as some kind of basement troll, the weird old guy who lurks below. But there is definitely something satisfying about the idea of redeeming and reclaiming that godforsaken space, tending to our roots in the troubled city. Urban renewal starting at home. Spring cleaning as psychic healing.

WHAT'S IN
A HOUSE NAME?

FRIENDS OF OURS NAMED THEIR HOUSE a few years ago. They decided to call it Hilltop, after Beatrice Potter's house, which they had visited on a trip to England. They admit that the name doesn't quite work since their house, while elevated, is not really on what you would call a hill, at least not the sort of hill that has anything so grand as a top and the name thus could just as easily apply to all the other houses on their road. But they liked all the old, named cottages and castles in England and felt the urge to pay tribute to Potter and her rabbits.

Americans have trouble with house names. We have no problem with naming children and pets—even our pet cars. Houses are something else. We tend to feel self-conscious giving names to our houses. Some people I know recently bought a house on a small, Spanish-speaking Caribbean island. The house is an unpretentious one of the local style, flat-roofed concrete; not waterfront, but with a nice little view of the sea. Some of the owners wanted to give the house a name to celebrate its virtues and express their affection for it: Flamboyant (after the large tree which frames the house), Wild Palms (for those forming part of the view). But others felt that doing so would make the house stand out as an immodest gringo upstart from its traditional neighborhood.

Giving a house a name suggests the hubris of self-conscious ownership, conspicuous possession. We fear being pretentious. When we do bestow a name, it is likely to be of the self-deprecating sort, a little joke on ourselves and on the tradition of naming itself. My brother-in-law says he developed his dislike of housenaming from his mother's name for their cottage on a lake in the Midwest: Shangri-Shack. You can see his point. This sort of cute irony is one way we have of simultaneously naming and distancing ourselves from the practice. Punning is another, as in one named cottage on Wellfleet's Mayo Beach: Brick-A-Dune.

One rather charmingly named house in town in a prominent spot at the top of an old road is Morning Glory. Part of the charm is in the name's modesty in opting to identify the house with a common flower instead of bragging about the 180 degree view of the harbor (that would have had to be done in Spanish—Buena Vista or some such; whoever heard of a house named Great View?). Right next to Morning Glory we have Morning After, so-named by a well-known young cutup-about-town. This classic example of the self-deprecating variety of house name is unique in my experience in playing on the name of its neighbor.

Good house names are those which, in avoiding both the sentimental and the clever, and other expressions of the personality of the namer, will stay with the house long after the particular owner bestowing the name is long gone. Such names, whether chosen consciously or not, often seem simply a result of the natural, communal process of giving directions to a place: the house at the top of the hill, the house with the red shutters, the house with the prominent display of morning glories, the House of the Seven Gables.

Of course such names work only with a stable society. What if an inheriting owner wanted a gable or two less or more? What if someone down the line got tired of producing that crop of morning glories every year? What if a U.S. president came along who wanted to do a bit of exterior decorating of the traditional residence? Big problem. (Certainly the White House is a name that transcends the individual resident. In fact the house name is often given instead of that of the prominent tenant, as in the common formulation "The White House issued a statement.")

A deterrent to naming in many contemporary settings is the master-planned development: too many houses looking too much like each other. Except in the case of famous residences or residences of the famous, traditional, appropriate naming assumes a setting sufficiently stable and intimate that every dwelling has a known location and distinct personality—like the places in Jane Austen's novels.

In the 1940s children's book *Homer Price*, by Robert McCloskey, there is a good-humored, lightly satirical chapter on the then newish phenomenon of tract homes. It is actually the pride of the developers in the book that all the houses are mass produced for efficiency and lower price and look as much alike on their flat, barren lots as Model T Fords coming off the assembly line, another achievement of American ingenuity. The only trouble is, the houses look so much alike that when the street sign man gets drunk and fails to get the signs up, the proud new owners can't find their way home. In such a setting, house names would be very useful in giving a touch of personality and distinction to the otherwise profoundly undistinguished. Of course, lacking objective architectural or topographical basis for names, the names would no doubt tend to be of the self-aggrandizing or gratuitous sort.

Perhaps our difficulty with house names is an index of the decline and fall of places. When houses stop having names by which we naturally refer to them, it means the town has gotten developed to the point where it is no longer possible for houses to have that desirable quality of having an acknowledged place in the local scheme of things. An extreme example of this is when people themselves, in certain dystopian views of the future, are given only numbers instead of names.

SUBMITTING
TO MAIN STREET

AFTER THE TERRIBLE ACCIDENT in late March
(two cars filled with five Wellfleet people smashing into
each other just over the line in Eastham), several other
accidents since then, and that freedom-loving fellow
American clocked at 107 going through Truro the other
night, I imagine I am not the only one thinking twice
before venturing out on the Route 6 Terrorbahn.

When duty calls me to the fray, I am trying very hard
to drive defensively, as the slogan goes, hoping to
establish around my car an aura of ponderous
responsibility that will act as a sort of shield while exuding
infectious patience. In this mode I think of myself as
imitating the country geezer in his old pickup, jes takin'
his time, not about to be stampeded by the goldurned
tourists.

Actually, I think I have become that geezer.

One thing became clear at the June 25 Eastham Town
Hall meeting on the future of Route 6—those troubled
about our vital artery are divided by two very different
ways of thinking about a solution. The traffic engineering
approach seems to be to smooth the flow, reduce curb
cuts, make the road as close as possible to limited access;
bypass the town if possible. One of Wellfleet's newly
elected selectmen makes it seem the only realistic, grown-

up thing to do: let an Interstate-style swath of highway sweep all the way to the tip of this narrow land.

Then there is the other approach. Wellfleet selectman David Ernst: "There should be very noticeable signage as soon as one enters from the Orleans rotary indicating that the driver is entering a residential area and the penalties [for speeding] are severe."

Alix Ritchie, Provincetown rep to the Cape Cod Commission: "Do whatever you can to remind people it's NOT a limited access highway."

Kevin Boyle, Eastham resident: "Make this main street a main street."

According to this approach, Route 6 past the rotary is not a highway at all and the problem is only in people continuing to make the mistake of driving as if it were. The problem is in the typical driver's feeling of entitlement. Cars can go 60, they want to go 60; they ought to be allowed to go 60. The problem is in our irritation on discovering that after the passivity of the pines and oaks that line the Mid-Cape Highway, here we have this town full of our considerably more active fellow human beings to deal with. How annoying.

Time was, back in the '40s and '50s, before the Interstate mentality took over, on a trip you had to go through every little town on the route. Cars slowed drastically at the town limits and submitted to the human pace of the town. The towns tamed the cars. Sure, it could be irritating. You were interested in "making good time," in pushing on to those tourist cabins at the end of the driving day. But it was just the way it was. Every highway turned into Main Street in town. As a reward for your patience you did get to make the acquaintance of the town, which was, after all, just as much a part of the trip as the trees and hills in between.

When I go into Wellfleet center (bypassed back in the '40s) I am often irritated by the summertime congestion, tourists fussing their way through the commercial strip looking for parking, pedestrians looking for chances to cross. Main Street presents itself mainly as an obstacle to the efficient pursuit of my personal business. But it seems to me this is less a problem of Main Street than of my attitude. Towns should tame cars. People should come before cars. Progress may be irritatingly slow through Wellfleet center, but I must say, if I lived in Eastham I would want Route 6 turned back into the Main Street it once was. I would not want cars sweeping through town as if I weren't there. I would want my human presence acknowledged. Eastham deserves a Main Street.

ω ω ω

When I was a kid I was taken by my grandparents to Chautauqua Institution, a religious and cultural community in western New York State. One of the most memorable things about the experience was Chautauqua's ban on automobiles. To get in you had to go through a main gate. You were allowed in to unload your belongings at your rental, but after that you had to keep your car in a large parking lot on the perimeter, a sort of car ghetto. Because of this, people, including lots of kids and older folks, could roam carefree along narrow roads and wide brick walks. The lack of autos was right up there with the art and music as one of the things that made this a truly civilized little town. They had a policy that put people before cars.

Closer to home, Provincetown is another place whose level of civilization is expressed as much in its auto scene as in its art and restaurant scene. Oh, sure, there are too many cars in Provincetown. There is a congested feel to things in the summer and parking gets harder and harder. The suggestion has been made more than once that cars be banished, Chautauqua-style, to a pen on the edge of town. But one of the pleasures of the present, unsegregated arrangement on Commercial Street is how, with cars and people mingling freely in the same space, the hardbodies, in a reversal of the usual situation, are dominated by the softbodies.

It's almost touching, the helplessness of the cars which venture down the strip, wading through the human morass. Their inability to accelerate, to break free, to terrorize all in their path—to act, that is, like cars—is one of the main features of the summertime scene. People strolling languidly, cars inching their way, fenders caressing thighs, hands patting cars on their rumps in an unusual intimacy—it's one of the things that makes Commercial Street such a truly civilized space.

It is a great tribute to human ingenuity to have invented a device that packs the power of many horses into a conveyance able to go many times the speed of the former vehicle. A great achievement. The great achievement now is to rein in those horses. It is as big a breakthrough to learn to use a machine with restraint as it is to unleash its potential in the first place.

The Outer Cape has always been an out-of-the-way place, not on anyone's beeline to anywhere, the ultimate cul-de-sac. Let's make a languid pace our gift to elsewhere, along with the oysters and the scenic beauty. One can imagine the bumper stickers: "Patience, Our Proudest Product." "Slow and Proud Of It." "Dare to be inefficient." "We Put People Before Cars."

MYSTERY FENCE
AT OLD PIER ROAD

NOT LONG AGO, WELLFLEET CITIZENS woke up
to find that a split rail fence had been installed right down
the middle of the turnaround at the end of Old Pier Road.

Old Pier is a short town road running along a marsh
and dead-ending, with a packed-sand turnaround, at a
beach on the inner harbor. It's not much of a road, not
much of a beach, and not many people use it; human
beachgoers are way outnumbered by the horseshoe crabs
who seem to favor the area. Nevertheless, it is a sweet
spot in its understated way, right down to the crumbling,
sand-blown road itself, which is frequently inundated by
the higher tides. It's one of the little things that make this
town what it is.

For close to a quarter of a century, I have moored a
small sailboat off the beach at the end of Old Pier Road at
half tide. It was upsetting to drive down there for a sail
one day and find this fence which, for no reason that I
could see, threatened my long-standing practice. How was
I supposed to turn around? Back all the way out to Cove
Road? A driveway only a 100 yards down offered an
alternative; but surely the town didn't mean to include a
private drive as part of public access?

Behind the new fence, where the sand had been
packed with ancient usage, a lot of loose sand had been

dumped, apparently to build up the adjacent dune. But it was the wrong color sand: instead of the greyish white of the original, the ocher tint of the backside dune. Alien sand had been dumped in my backup place.

Who did this and why? Had this been all the time not a public access but private property? I decided I better go to the next selectmen's meeting to present my grievance and find out the story. At the open session of the meeting I felt nervous in my role of lone defender (as I had imagined it) of a piece of town I cared about. But I was surprised and encouraged to find the room full of others who for one reason or another were outraged at this fence appearing in the middle of what was quickly determined was indeed a town right-of-way. Shellfishermen objected to the town selling permits and eliminating access. Others, like me, had aesthetic or recreational reasons for feeling aggrieved. Some just didn't like on principle the idea of having public access for all practical purposes eliminated without due process.

The story has a happy ending. In response to the public outcry, the selectmen ordered that hearing be convened forthwith to get to the bottom of the matter and make a recommendation. Apparently—the story is still a bit murky to me, despite some effort spent trying to understand it—an informal coalition of conservationists and local owners were behind the DPW's installation of the offending fence. Within a few weeks of its appearance it was whisked away, case closed.

However this mistake—if that's the right word for it—came to be made, surely there is a lesson to be learned here of the "If it ain't broke, don't fix it" variety. As far as I can tell, there never was a problem at the end of Old Pier Road, at least not a problem for most of us who in fact used it. What went on there over the years, the human usage, was appropriate and benign, with the exception of the occasional parking jam during low tides in shellfishing season, an inconvenience the shellfishermen themselves seemed able to live with. Over many, many years there, the access road and the traditional activities of light boating, shellfishing and beach strolling seemed a pretty good fit for each other.

Malls, superhighways, highrises and largescale housing developments have understandably made us suspicious of all human activity in our time. But Wellfleet's unique charm owes as much to traditional, appropriate human practice—its houses, sand roads, footpaths, the working of the flats—as to our beautiful natural setting. Traditional use of Old Pier Road is part of that charm.

Those who put the DPW up to monkeying with public access were motivated by a certain sort of concern for the area. But it was a rather abstract concern: save a dune, save the marsh, conserve wild space and the rest of the slogans. It is hard to believe anyone with much actual history with the place would have come up with this solution—including that inappropriately tinted sand.

As one of its citizen-owners, I am glad to have Old Pier Road back again, more or less intact. It has a fussed-over look it didn't have before, but I'm sure with time and winter storms it will be pretty much back to normal by next spring. The intense focus on this hitherto unobtrusive spot makes me nervous. But some good may come of it. Maybe the public scrutiny helps us know a little better what we value about our town, and why we value it.

FAIRWEATHER SAILOR

THIS YEAR THE FALL RITUAL of taking my boat out of the water provided a humbling perspective on my fairweather sailing.

For years I have sailed a 13 foot sailboat in Wellfleet harbor. I keep it moored off an inner harbor beach at half tide. I act as my own dinghy, wading or swimming, when need be, out to retrieve the boat, mostly because keeping a dinghy to service what is essentially a dinghy itself seems overkill.

The harbor and this boat seem about the right size for each other. In summer the typical fairweather southwesterlies of 15-20 knots is all the wind we can handle. At times it makes sailing a bit too much of a workout with all the jumping up and down and hiking out needed to keep the boat level. But many days, too, when the wind is light, I have been known to catnap at the tiller to the gentle motion of the boat barely ghosting along.

A big adventure on a nice hot day in summer is to head over to Great Island, the hilly sandbar that protects us from Cape Cod Bay and make a landing, always with a little of the feeling of discovering an exotic shore. We pull up on the beach, which is usually empty enough to impart just a bit of the flavor of Crusoe or Swiss Family Robinson making their landfalls. Keeping an eye on the tide to prevent getting stranded, we spread a blanket, eat sandwiches and drink a beer from the cooler.

These are the pleasures of summertime, fairweather sailing.

On blissful, calm mornings, before the winds are up, I have been witness to creatures of the deep, serious creatures such as sharks or porpoises or the small whale known as blackfish breaking the glassy surface, letting you know there is another world down there, beneath the sea's mirror surface.

But for the most part I am like the seagazers in Frost's poem, who look "neither out far nor in deep." I am content not to sail out beyond our snug harbor and to glide on the surface of the sea, leaving the depths to others.

At best my sailing is but a flirtation with the elements.

This year I waited too long into the fall to get the boat out. I meant to get it out by Columbus Day, but I kept hoping for one last sail. Keeping the sailing possibility alive is one way of prolonging summer—or, I suppose you could say, of denying the oncoming of winter. And then the weather turned and what with storms or the tide schedule or my personal schedule, suddenly it was November and more winter than summer. For weeks I hadn't been for a sail, had visited the boat only to bail it out.

I scheduled the takeout for three hours after high tide, when there should be still a couple of feet of water under the boat, but no more, not wanting to have to swim to fetch the boat. As it was, the wade to the mooring, up to my knees, was shockingly cold. The harbor in summer is like soup, the warmest of our various swimming possibilities. I hadn't thought it could get so cold in the few weeks since summer. It made my legs ache so badly that I thought: much more of this and I wouldn't be able to stand it, although I don't really know what that means.

I needed to sail only a short distance from my mooring over to the ramp off the pier, a 10 minute sail at most, and with the keen breeze out of the north or northwest and my bare feet still numb from wading, there was little temptation to dawdle, to extract from necessity that one last pleasure cruise.

The autumn wind was strong enough and, coming off the land, irregular enough that there was an unusual urgency in keeping the boat upright. In summer I don't fear the prospect of capsizing. The water I would be pitched into would be as welcoming an environment as the air. But the menace of that November water was still in my bones, in my mind. It was a tense little sail and I was very happy when the boat, after just a bit more wading, was safely up on its trailer and stowed in a corner of our driveway.

This stressful sail got this fairweather sailor thinking about old seafaring Wellfleet, all those who had made the sea their year-round business. About fishermen who go far out to the banks over the freezing water, risking storms, to get fish; or even just the draggers who go in circles in the harbor on cold autumn and winter days. We share a town, a harbor, but ours are two different worlds.

SHARING WORDS

WELLFLEET HAS BEEN THROUGH a couple of years of nasty politics, a time which has left many wondering whether this town can still run itself, whether we should just hand it over to professionals—if we could just agree on the right professional to hand it over to. Anyone dropping in on tense, divisive selectmen's meetings over recent months might be excused for wondering just what we mean in applying the word "community" to ourselves as often as we do.

But a memorial service held in the Congregational church on a January morning would be a perfect explanation of what is meant by that no doubt overused term.

The purpose of this memorial service was impossibly ambitious: to somehow help the parents, friends and many others concerned cope with one of the bleakest of all events, the death of a young person, in this case the death by cancer of 19-year-old Jesse, son of Kristin and Dennis—and also, in some meaningful sense, a son of Wellfleet.

I am sure I was not the only one feeling, as we approached the church, that, really, there is no comfort to be offered to these parents, no comfort to be had out of this situation. Just grief. And there was plenty of grieving.

The large church was full to overflowing with people whom this
death touched in one way or another.

The feeling in the room was obvious everywhere you looked, the feeling that here was a loss too deep and unfair to be borne. And yet somehow, the sheer accumulation of all that sorrow in that big, high ceilinged space became a palpable presence embracing us all, swathing us all in whatever comfort can be had from shared grief.

And then there were the words. On the card handed us at the door, a quote from *Romeo and Juliet*:

Take him and cut him out in little stars
And he will make the face of heaven so fine
That the world will be in love with night...

Words so moving to me at that moment: perfect words to help in imagining the lost one into continued existence of some sort, at least in the feelings of others. Words 400 years old, and it's as if they had been written just for this occasion.

There were the words of Jesse's friend Dan spoken from the front of the room in a surprisingly mature voice, deep and soft, words just able to contain their feeling, words from his last entry in Jesse's journal read to Jesse, on which we were, it felt, privileged to eavesdrop. (I wished for my son such a friend, that my son be such a friend to such a friend.)

Many of the words were about the local theme of connection to nature. There was a quote from Rachel Carson about "this place of the meeting of land and water" and "that intricate fabric of life by which one creature is linked to another, and each with its surroundings." And again, how perfectly fitting, given this young man's lifelong intimacy with this watery place, to remind us of our implicit connection to him through this shared medium of the water that is all around, that permeates our town, our lives.

There were stories from Jesse's life, some of them producing the blessing of laughter. There were the words and music of a song for the occasion. You could feel in all the words the effort to maintain connection with the lost one, to find some legitimate way to hold on to him. It is as

if with the right words we would indeed keep Jesse alive in our hearts, in the collective heart.

And you could feel the connection among those left behind. It was as if the community, by its ongoing presence, would not let Kristin and Dennis drift away from the communal mainland. Bereft they might be, but not alone, not lost, if this gathering had anything to say about it. And it had a lot to say about it. The words and the feeling in the words held out, one felt—one fervently hoped—possibilities of healing for Kristin and Dennis, for all of us. Here was the possibility of a non-theistic continuity, of making the loss less sheer, less insupportable.

I found myself feeling quite grateful to the speakers and writers of those words. What if Shakespeare had not written precisely those words from *Romeo and Juliet?* What if no one had thought to look for them there? What if Jesse's friend had been too overcome to speak his love for his friend? What if Stack had not been there to sing that song?

Toward the end the minister spoke the old words: "now may the peace that passeth understanding abide with us..." I've never really paid much attention to that familiar benediction before, not being a religious sort, but I must say it went right to the point of this day. Suddenly I saw that in those words was exactly what I needed: peace that goes beyond my rational understanding of this death as unforgiveably cruel.

And finally the minister said "it's over folks," or words to that effect, sensing, I thought, something in that room that did not want to stop ever, as if just continuing the service, holding Jesse with our feelings and words in our midst, we wouldn't have to go on without him. He was saying, gently, let him go now. Again, simple words, ones that might well not have been spoken, but important.

I remind myself of the terrible limits to how much we can help each other in the face of something like this. It is hard to know how much solace Jesse's parents ended up taking away from this ritual gathering. But if community can have a healing effect, can to any extent alleviate the pain, mitigate the loss, surely this would be the way.

SELF-DOUBT HERE IN THE MIDDLE PERIOD OF MALL PROLIFERATION

THERE'S AN ARTICLE on the Wellfleet Town Meeting warrant proposing to tear down the old police and fire station. It has, they say, "deteriorated to the point of collapse, is a hazard to public safety" and needs to come down. Sounds like a proper thing to do. Why don't I feel happier at the prospect?

It's not as if this were an architectural gem. It is not even all that old; with its cracking shingles, flaking trim and cockeyed doors, it looks older than its early '40s vintage. So why shed a tear over an old, falling-down building? Because an old building, even one that no longer fills its original function, does embody valuable continuity. This is a town in which simple longevity means something—in people, trees, buildings. It is part of a whole scheme of things that seems quite satisfactory the way it is. You want to be careful tinkering with parts of a good arrangement. Maybe we owe something to the familiar just because it is familiar. (Come to think of it, this building is not any older than I am; maybe I'm just a little sensitive to its being so unceremoniously discarded.)

But there is something else in my reluctance to see this old building get knocked down and carted away. A couple of years ago, a town committee I serve on was looking at the Mooney building near the old railroad trestle over

Duck Creek (talk about rotting old structures that occupy a place in one's heart). The idea was for the town to buy the building, no longer used by the oil company whose name it bears, and make it into something useful and relevant—a little museum of our harbor and fishing industry, perhaps, maybe even a center for the study of aquaculture. A certain part of the motivation was to keep the property out of the hands of people who might, for profit, do something not so interesting and helpful with it, just to make money. But even though our committee had only the best motives, I never quite trusted that whatever new thing we came up with, requiring either renovation of the existing building or a new building rising out of the demolition of the old, would be as appropriate to its setting, as full of character as the one we have all grown used to.

As in the case of the doomed police/fire station, it's not that this overgrown shack, with its shallow pitched roof and garish red shingles and flanked by several huge tanks (possibly seeping pollution), was anything but an eyesore in the usual sense of the term. And yet I realized I would be more comfortable just letting it continue its present life as ramshackle home to various craftsfolk until, over many decades, it slowly decayed into just another of the derelicts of our harbor margins. Here I was sitting on a committee doing its best to come up with forms of what we call nowadays Appropriate Development (as opposed to chain stores, malls, and other agents of the devil waiting to pounce on a small, unsuspecting town), but I had to admit that some part of me was mistrustful of even appropriate development—didn't, in fact, want any development at all.

Almost certainly, old-timey Cape Codders were not charmed by their own contructed world the way we are. So I suppose we must at least entertain the notion that our cul de sac housing, highway clutter and malls will, in ways beyond our present ken, look charmingly old fashioned to our great-great-grandchildren. It is entirely possible, I suppose, that the Cape Cod Mall's classic banality will in a generation or two be seen, through a haze of nostalgia, as a gem of the Middle Period of Mall Proliferation.

I don't look forward to the time, if it ever comes, when our leaning tower (formerly of pizza) is made to conform to building code requirements of plumbness, the stumps of the old Chequesett Hotel extracted from the Mayo Beach flats like rotten teeth, our harbor edges purged of all the decaying boats that make walking there so interesting. I realize all this affection for decay and mistrust of the new is not an attitude which can be indulged, beyond a point. A building becomes unsafe, it needs to come down. We do not have the luxury of refusing to be as creative as we can be in coming up with a new form of life to take the place of the old.

YEE HAW

I WAS WAITING TO BE SERVED at a local store the other day when I overheard a happy man. He was updating a friend, whom he apparently had not seen for a while, on his work life: "Yeah, I'm workin' over at that development in the woods. My boss has a few houses going over there. When we're finished there we go down to Harwich. He's got a bunch more set to go down there. Then back up to Eastham. We're goin' flat out, 6 days a week, puttin' in as many hours as there is daylight. Oh, yeah, we're havin' a great time... and the money ain't bad either."

The image that sprang to mind was that of Wimpy, of the Popeye cartoons, salivating in front of a big plate of burgers. In this case the burgers were Cod burgers. The joy in this carpenter's life, the sparkle in his eye, the spring in his step was in gobbling up, as enthusiastically as possible ... the Cape—your Cape, my Cape, his own Cape.

Now, as a sometime builder myself, I can appreciate where this good ole boy is coming from. It does feel good to be out in the woods on a nice spring day building a house. Radio blasting, jokes flying, it feels mighty free and easy to be out there swinging a hammer, popping nails with your nailgun and seeing the big effects as the frame goes up. Standing up framed walls in the woods—why it's like making giant sculpture on instant display. It's a great life, with some of the same freedom, rare enough in modern paper-shuffling, number-crunching America, of the old frontier.

I can understand it, I can appreciate it, both the work and the bucks it puts in the pocket. Building one house feels good; building a whole bunch of houses must really be a high. But there is no question: this guy and his enthusiasm for transforming forest into suburban style housing is a big problem these days, in the era of Land Bank Consciousness.

Mr. and Mrs. Jones of the Boston or New Jersey suburbs may want a new house, most likely a second home for seasonal use until a possible retirement down the road. The Cape does not need a bunch of new houses (as the Joneses will find out as soon as they've got theirs).

Thoughtless, pro-growth mentality might have been perfectly appropriate a few decades back, when there was more wide open space than there were locals to make a dent in it (although yes, sooner or later, it led to our present predicament). It is, I suppose, an example of the great American can-do attitude, the attitude that built America, won the west.

But here and now, at this point in our history, this guy is a living contradiction. His construction feels like destruction to most of us. His freedom means crowding and stress to the great majority. His pro-growth voraciousness, however colorful, however innocent, is a form of pollution.

At the risk of committing metaphorical pollution, this carpenter reminded me of all those old westerns in which the oldtime gunslingers and other Real Men of the open range run smack into the future in the form of law-abiding townspeople who have no use for their old bust-em-up, shoot-em-up ways, even if those ways had come in mighty handy in getting the towns started.

He reminds me of the cowboy-bombardier in the film *Dr. Strangelove (Or How I Learned to Stop Worrying and Love the Bomb)* who at the end of the movie jumps on the A-bomb as it is released over the USSR, and rides it as if it were a bucking bronco. Yee-hawww, yee-hawww he yells, waving his ten gallon hat, as he plummets—and with him, the rest of mankind—to doomsday.

NATURAL SOCIALISM

IN A BOOK ON THE CREATION of the Cape Cod National Seashore I came upon a paragraph explaining that in the pre-Seashore 1950s, "the owners of Jeremy Point in Wellfleet had offered some 500 acres to the Audubon Society." All of Great Island, it continues, was "eventually purchased from the Henderson family by the United States."

For some reason I found this shocking to read. Great Island, every Wellfleetian's western horizon, three miles of wooded hills and sandbar, had been private property? No doubt in some sense I knew this. Of course it had been; everything is private property unless made into a park. But I guess I have gotten used to the idea of Great Island as not so much National Park as just open space. Public land. A place one feels free to take a walk.

Great Island has all my days here seemed too wild, raw, simply too much of the sea and sky to belong to anyone. It seems so right that it belongs to all of us as a common resource and treasure. So natural. It seems slightly obscene now to think of it as having been owned.

I've read that back in the '40s and '50s Mrs. Henderson used to patrol her property with a gun to keep off trespassers—the likes of you and me. Back in the good old days, taking a walk out to Jeremy Point wasn't the tame affair it has become. What if, in their pursuit of happiness, the Hendersons had decided to line the bay and harbor with highrise hotels? Strip malls? Made it into an exclusive country club?

When I was growing up in Westchester County, New York, the Long Island Sound waterfront was something glimpsed behind large houses and well kept lawns and fences. In a sense the water itself was owned by the wealthy people in those houses, since they owned the access.

One of the crucial differences between Martha's Vineyard, where various members of my extended family have seen fit to locate, and Wellfleet is that much of the Vineyard coastline is off limits, owned and patrolled by wealthy landholders, where here virtually all the natural treasures are open to all. Much of the Vineyard feels like a preserve of the wealthy.

In the late '50s when the Seashore legislature was being debated in local hearings and in Washington, the idea was very controversial. Most Outer Cape towns opposed it. Why would Wellfleet residents strongly oppose something that would enable them to take a walk on Mrs. Henderson's property without the adventure of having her come charging at them with her gun? Why did people oppose what seems like their own self-interest? A major factor, no doubt, was the understandable feeling locally that the proposed park would not be theirs and their neighbors' so much as a "national treasure" reserved for the "American people," in the words of the Washington politicians, whereas locals had always seen it as theirs, their town. And if the 60% of town under consideration by the Park would otherwise be developed and the profits reaped by some rich s.o.b., at least it was their s.o.b., a local, a neighbor. It would be in the family, in a way. Better take your chances with Mrs. H's aim than with a bunch of Washington politicians and being treasured to death by hordes of fellow Americans.

On the other hand, from the perspective of the contemporary beneficiary of the Seashore intervention, didn't that alien legislation affirm and guarantee another right that seems just as identified from the beginning with this town—our access to all the large effects of our town—our beaches and ponds and woods?

In one sense "we" lost that 60% or so of our town—lost the individual right to possess it; in another sense we all got it back—the full recreational use of it. The Seashore did not take it from the town (pack it up and ship it elsewhere) but bought it from the few who owned it and gave it to all of us (including the former owners). It's a great bargain. Even Ted Turner could not put together a Cape ranch such as is available to all of us.

Ours is a private property society and so private property seems perfectly natural, if awfully inconvenient if you are a not-so-wealthy kid from an inland town trying to get to Long Island Sound for a swim on a hot day. When it comes to natural rights, when you think about it, public land has a much longer history than the right to buy, own and dispose of it. Until Europeans arrived on these shores it had never occurred to anyone to buy or own or sell the land this town occupies. The European way of buying and selling dominated for three centuries, a short time in the big picture. Now, thanks to a bit of governmental socialism, we are back to the ancient tradition of public, universal access and use.

The Seashore has kept alive in us the sense, long extinguished in other parts of the country (like my childhood terrain) of the naturalness of open space, of land just there for the walking on, the swimming in, the dreaming about. The irony is that it took regulation and legislation to create the semblance of free, unregulated space.

The Park is a wonderful gift—for all Americans, no doubt, as the founders kept saying; but most of all for us who live here all the time.

VIEQUES' NAVY BASE, OUR NATIONAL PARK

I SHARE WITH A SURPRISING NUMBER of other Outer Cape Codders a connection with the small island of Vieques, off the east coast of Puerto Rico. At times you run into so many friends and neighbors there it can seem like a Caribbean outpost of the Cape.

Vieques is actually a lot like the Outer Cape: laid-back, funky, relatively undeveloped, with a motley, creative gringo (read washashore) community. Another similarity is our shared condition of being an occupied, colonized place. 40 years ago the Congress voted into law the National Seashore, claiming for the people of the United States, as a national treasure, about two-thirds of the area—the beaches, ponds, woods that our towns and townspeople had hitherto thought of as their own.

About 60 years ago the feds claimed about 75 percent of the island of Vieques as a Navy base. World War II was in its early stages and not going well for our allies in Europe. The intention was to build a breakwater the seven miles from Vieques to mainland Puerto Rico, creating a huge artificial harbor in which, if England were to fall to the Nazis, the entire British fleet could be accommodated. You can still go fishing or take a walk on the mile long pier that was as far as they got with that project.

The war went better, the idea of the monster harbor was dropped. But the Navy, having herded citizens, by legal if highhanded means, into the central quarter of the island, stayed on as a base. Today it is used periodically for maneuvers and bombing practice, intensified recently as we seemed headed for another war with Iraq.

Locals in both places still resent the outside interference in their affairs; they feel gypped in the way in which they lost potential profits in their property.

Surely, you say, the comparison between our National Seashore and Vieques' occupation by the Navy is deeply flawed by the great differences between the two federal presences. The Navy is about bombing and making war; the Seashore is a peaceful, quiet presence protecting the environment and providing recreation.

But the fact is the two function in much the same way. The main effect of both is to remove private property from the possibility of development. That was the complaint about the Seashore in the 50s; it is still the complaint of some contemporary Viequensies: the Navy is preventing development of our island and keeping our citizens impoverished. For the most part the Navy acts as a nature preserve and park. Except for the tip of the island which gets blasted to smithereens, and a few earthen mounds of buried ordnance, nature lies fallow there as in our park. Most of the time people are allowed to drive onto the base for swimming and other recreation.

The bombing and occasional insensitive treatment of fishermen are serious annoyances but then Outer Cape locals have their complaints about insenstivity on the part of the federal occupiers of our towns, with ongoing battles over skating, dogs, and nudity.

A lot of people in both places basically approve the situation, not because it could not be better, but because it could be much worse—because we fear the consequences of the removal of the occupying force.

Most people now approve of the National Seashore, I gather, despite some unfairness in its handling of the original takeover and recurrent management insensitivity, because it seems clear to most of us that had citizens gone on managing their own towns the Outer Cape would now be a mess. Much that many of us like about the area would be lost. It would not be the place we love.

There is an indigenous movement to get rid of the Navy on Vieques. One sees "Navy afuera"—Navy out!—sprayed on roads and walls. The gripes are more serious, clearly. (Picture south Wellfleet, say, being heavily bombed a few weeks a year with possible pollution problems, as has been found on Upcape military bases). But the movement is hampered by a perception shared by many—a majority of the gringo community but also some of the local Viequensie population—that if the Navy were to withdraw, development like that just across the water in Fajardo, high rises, all-inclusive resorts, and malls would overwhelm the island and island life.

Maybe some people would have more money, but everybody would lose the slowly paced, peaceful place with traditional values they have enjoyed. (The island is known for its *paso fino* horses which roam the fields and are still ridden bareback through the streets.) It is feared that present day Viequensies would sell the soul of their island for a mess of pottage.

We all love freedom; we don't like regulation from outside. But when it comes down to it, when faced with a choice of colonialism in the form of federal takeover and colonialism in the form of bigtime corporate money and power, a lot of us are inclined to trust the feds. Even bombs do less damage than developers' ambitions. In other words, we look to the outside—to ourselves in the form of our government—to save us from ourselves in the form of capitalists.

[NOTE: *In April 1999, the accidental killing of a local Navy worker sparked a renewed effort to force the Navy to leave. Protesters occupied the bombing site for months, preventing its use and claims of the public health hazard posed by the bombing received more publicity than ever, leading President Clinton to sign an agreement that the Navy would leave permanently by 2002. The Navy's occupation of the western portion of the island ended at the specified time and jurisdiction divided amongst the Department of the Interior, the government of Vieques and local conservation groups. The end of military presence in the eastern portion of the island, the actual bombing range, is promised for 2003.*]

FRAUGHT WITH APPRECIATION

THERE WE WERE a couple of weeks ago going against
the grain: heading toward the bridge while everyone else
in the world was cramming onto the Cape. The cars in
the downcape lanes were of course creeping along.   But
our pleasure in our own easy going was considerably
undermined by knowing that our zippy pace was only
speeding us toward, of all dubious midsummer
destinations, Syracuse (actually a small 'burb to the south
of it).   The Cape-bound cars might have been stuck in
traffic but they had logic on their side: where you want to
be in early August is here, not anywhere else.

Greater Syracuse clearly is not a destination resort, as I
understand that term: a place people go for its intrinsic
virtues. My wife's mother has chosen to live in the
Syracuse area and it is not the charm of the area but her
own considerable charm and family ties that take any of
us there. We arrive in the middle of (what else?) a heat
wave, joking nervously: Where do they keep the ocean?
But I am discovering that even if you wouldn't exactly
choose to go there without an ulterior motive—in fact,
precisely because you wouldn't and neither would anyone
else—upstate New York has one charm we don't have, or
haven't had   for a long time: the charm of unselfcon-

sciousness. The charm of not being known for its charm. The virtue of having no particular virtues.

I did some running and walking along farm roads near my mother-in-law's house and found an unexpected source of happiness in the innocence of those fields sufficiently beyond the sprawl of Syracuse to be of no interest (at present) to developers, a land with no ocean or mountains to attract tourists. Half of it was not even under cultivation. No Open Space Com or Land Bank or Conservation Trust competed for it with evil developers and realtors. Even if the occasional lumpish trophy house had fouled a former cornfield, there seemed enough of these undistinguished hills to squander a few acres here or there without everyone getting all uptight about it.

Increasingly our beautiful Outer Cape seems tainted or burdened by of all things its very value, by our appreciation of it, by all the uproar over its preservation. Our concern about keeping it unpolluted itself becomes a form of pollution. The word *fraught* has been in my mind recently in relation to our narrow land. The dictionary defines fraught as charged, laden, freighted (of which it is the older English form)—usually with something negative, as in "fraught with difficulty." There is a quality to life on the Outer Cape that can be called fraught—fraught, in our case with appreciation, cherishing, concern.

Another word—*precious*. We are so precious, in the good sense—so wonderful, of such high value, so cherished—that we become precious in the other, pejorative sense: too self-conscious, affected, cloying. The word *appreciation* itself has an instructive double meaning. Our appreciation of this territory of ours becomes inextricably intertwined with and tainted by the appreciation of the other, monetary, exploitative sense.

So it was indeed a vacation we took, our against-the-grain idyll in upstate New York, not to a change of scenery, as ocean people who want to breathe from mountaintops once in a while, not to more pristine versions of ourselves like downeast Maine, but to the unsung, the undistinguished, the un-sought-after. A vacation from the fraughtness of the Outer Cape.

The Cape is home, of course, and underneath all the fussing, exploiting, buying and selling with which we are fraught the land itself remains wonderful and you can, in blessed, unlooked-for moments get down or back to that quality. But it is good to know that America is a big country and that there is still a lot of the other, unfraught land left.

THE PLUGGED
AND THE UNPLUGGED

HAS EVERYONE BY NOW heard the story (from Krakauer's *Into Thin Air*) of that guy near the summit of Mt. Everest simultaneously schmoozing on the phone with his wife several thousand miles away and freezing to death in one of the world's most out-of-the-way places? It is a story just slightly more bizarre than it is heart-rending. An image, somehow, for our time.

I preferred thinking of Everest as an off-the-grid sort of place. In fact, I have always liked to think of the Outer Cape as an off-the-grid place, at least compared with the burbs and urbs we washashores left behind. It always seemed an essential virtue of this ultimate cul de sac. But that virtue has been seriously eroded in the last decade or two by cable TV, computers and cell phones.

When we first built our house in the early '80s the only available reception, from antennas, was so miserable that a small black and white TV set was the only sensible choice. Who would want to make a large-screen, color display of such a lousy signal? When we moved here fulltime we were making a choice—the constraints of this Outer Cape village over the cable-enabled global village of which McLuhan wrote. Now with cable hookup available even in my sparsely populated sand road neighborhood I spend a certain part of each week in complete transcendence of this remote place, happily watching football or sitcoms with millions of my fellow Americans.

I had an experience the other day which put to the test my own commitment to the virtues of the unplugged.

I was returning in late afternoon from a mid-September sail to Great Island in our little boat with my son and a friend of his when, as it sometimes does this time of day, the light wind became fitful, and finally died altogether. We were not far from our mooring, but in a sailboat with no wind, with no auxiliary power except a pair of cheap plastic paddles and something of an adverse current, that mile or so could take a while.

No doubt, I found myself thinking, this is the sort of situation when some people would be using their cell phone and feeling mighty happy to have one.

In fact, I had to admit, as the sun dropped toward the humps of Great Island and lost its warmth, my wet toes grew cold and the boys started to complain, in fact I would myself be tempted, if I had one.

Yessir, I said to myself as just a suggestion of crisis mentality settled over our little outing, this is exactly the sort of problem, cell phone advocates would be saying, that cell phones were made to solve. I could have called up first of all to tell my wife what was happening, to allay any worries; she could have called the other kid's parents. As with the fellow expiring on top of Everest, it would have been comforting, somehow, to have that connection to hearth and home. I could, in fact, have had her meet us at the closest beach where we could have left the boat anchored overnight, to be retrieved the next day when it would no doubt be warmer and the wind blowing.

As it was, we applied our little plastic oars, drifted in on the occasional whisper of breeze. It took way too long and was dark and chilly when we arrived. My wife had been on the point of calling the police when we finally arrived home an hour after dark.

On the positive side, there was a spectacular sunset. I realized I had never before been on the water to see the sun go down. We had greater leisure to follow its progress than one usually gives oneself. The quality of the evening stillness was another perk. In the growing dusk we spied a dorsal fin doing a strange sort of dance toward us. A seagoing sunfish, we were told later. An apparition of that darkling moment.

All-in-all, not the sort of sail you would ever plan. Definitely on the inconvenient side. And yet in my book the virtues of being unplugged won out over the discomforts. I think this sail might have ended up being my son's favorite precisely because it had a bit of the feeling of an adventure. Adventures tend to be inconvenient.

Of course even if you personally disdain to use these gadgets the experience is fundamentally altered, because now it is your choice to risk getting becalmed, your choice to be out of touch. Those presiding over supper at home are likely, in this new era of super connectedness, to be less indulgent of the sailor's excuses.

A JUICE
BY ANY OTHER NAME

HAVE YOU TRIED Wellfleet Farms brand juice, the latest Ocean Spray marketing gambit? We tried the cranberry and key lime, trying hard to discern a hint of our town in the flavor of that juice, but failed.

Just what flavor juice might be considered to capture the essence of our town, as margaritas or pina coladas are associated with tropical islands? I don't know. Clam juice perhaps; low tide cocktail. It is possible no juice gets it just right.

What's in a name, our name? Apparently a juice by any other name, even the name of a town that actually grows cranberries or key limes, would not taste as sweet. Wellfleet is a nice clean, wholesome name. Something about all those e's, the suggestion of harbor breezes and general well-being.

Not wholesome enough, apparently. Hence the puzzling addition of "Farms," which would make more sense if this were Ohio or Iowa rather than a place whose average topsoil is a 6-inch layer of leaves and pine needles over sandbar. Wellfleet Flats or something actually more typical of this place I guess just wouldn't sell juice.

I suppose the idea is that tourists, pining away for summer weeks spent here, will pluck that name from grocery shelves for a hit of the magic that we are—

summer magic in a bottle. It will really be the name and their associations with it that they will be imbibing; the juice itself will be irrelevant. It will be, as those ad guys like to say, the sizzle, not the steak.

If Wellfleet oysters, why not Wellfleet juice? The difference of course is that Wellfleet when applied to our most famous product is just an adjective, not a brand name and refers to a product actually found here in abundance, a product that characterizes the town.

The hype on the juice bottle claims our fair town has been famous for its cranberries for over 100 years, But that's certainly not true of the 40 years out of that 100 I am personally aware of. According to a company P.R. spokesman I consulted, cranberries in Wellfleet Farms juice come from as far away as Vancouver, British Columbia as well as from New Jersey, whose image is such I can see the company not wanting its name associated with the product. (Newark Farms? Hohokus or Paramus Farms? I don't think so). It seems our good name is, of all things, being used to create a false impression.

I notice that "Wellfleet Farms" is a registered trademark, meaning that no one besides Ocean Spray can now use that label on a product, even one actually grown here. How can Ocean Spray just appropriate our name like this? I guess if an enterprising guy can trademark "year 2000," a phrase on every tongue you would think surely would be inalienable, common property (and I read this has happened), they can lasso our name.

Did someone in Town Hall grant permission to the company in our behalf? As citizens and taxpayers of this town whose name and fame are being capitalized on, can we all look forward to getting royalty checks in the mail on a regular basis? If they are going to use us to help sell their juice, the least they can do is give us a share of the profits.

SEEING OUR HOUSES AS OTHERS SEE THEM

I WAS HANGING OUT at the Wellfleet Planning Board meeting the other night, waiting for all hell to break loose on the cell tower front (the PB is where it's at in town on a Wednesday night these months, as sad as that may seem) when a whole other issue caught my attention.

A woman lawyer from the big city approached the board to argue that if her neighbors were allowed, as the PB was contemplating, to site their house on their lot where they wanted to site it, it would grievously encroach on her scene. Where now she has a view of trees, there would be a view of a house looming over her. Then the neighbors got up and said that if they built it elsewhere they would have the expense of an engineered septic system and other hardships. As these two parties confronted each other bitterly it was hard to see a happy conclusion of any sort to the situation. It was easy to predict years of Hatfield-and-McCoy-style unpleasantness.

I am aware of a number of such stories. Elsewhere in Wellfleet: Party A built a house maybe 20 years ago as a second, seasonal home. Party B built more recently cheek-by-jowl with the existing house of Party A and moved here fulltime. Eventually Party A moved here fulltime and Party B, apparently miffed to have people living fulltime in the house they had built so close to and whose windows looked right into their windows, hasn't spoken to them since, over 10 years.

Another situation of this sort: a family built their house as far to the back of their lot as possible to maximize privacy. On the other side of that back line was a sizeable chunk of unsubdivided acreage. When, 15 years later, those woods were transformed into a 20 house development, the new house on the lot closest to the original family was built looming over the pre-existing house, its deck overlooking the latter's backyard.

When the new family, on visits to the house abuilding, started to get the idea, they expressed dismay: Oh, we feel terrible. Our house is so close. It was as if the result brought about by their builder were a complete surprise to them. The architectural remedy to this architected intimacy was a very tall fence, cost split by both parties, to restore a semblance of privacy.

Another example: in Truro someone paid a pretty penny for a lot with a big bay view and of course built a big, two story house proportionate with the price of the lot and sited to maximize the big view. Unfortunately the logical site for the house in terms of view substituted a view of the new house for the view of the bay which the existing house had for many years before enjoyed from a bit farther back. The neighbor couldn't do anything about the house but sued over a proposed rooftop deck and held up the project for a couple of years. Lawsuits are known to be a bad way to get to know your neighbors.

It's funny. When we enter a situation we think of as social—say a party—we usually are very sensitive what impression we make on others with our dress, our body language, what we say. We get a sense of what's going on and find a way of relating. We are very careful not to thrust ourselves where or in ways not wanted. Same goes at the more secluded of our local ponds. The unspoken code is that everyone goes there for a quiet time with some privacy and when you arrive, as a new party, if at all possible you do not flop your blanket right next to a party already in residence. But when it comes to the biggest impression we will ever make, the largest and most permanent effect we will ever have on our social environment, that extension of us called a house, all sensitivity flies out the window. I guess it is overriden by our ideas about private property: Hey, this is my property, I paid for it, and I'll build wherever and however I please on it.

There may have been a time when this town was so rural and houses so spaced that such an attitude made no difference. These days it behooves us all to temper our architectural ambitions with some social sensitivity— to realize that neighborliness is in fact or ought to be an aspect of house design. You are not just building a house, you are beginning to construct a relationship with your neighbors—for better or worse, depending on the choices you make.

The pre-existing house—your neighbor's house—is a fait accompli. Just like the people already settled at pondside when you arrive, it has certain rights, just because it is there. You were not there when they made their siting and design decisions. They are there when you make yours. Do not ignore their house, do not ignore them.

It would be a good idea, before designing your house, to go over and meet your neighbors, talk to them, and most importantly, stand in the place from which they will be looking at your new house and get some idea of what they will see. As much as is practical, given the restrictions of setbacks, septic and well locations, design what you would want to see from their point of view, paying particular attention to how close and how tall you build (will your house seem to loom over or one-up theirs?). Design, in other words, not just with your own view in mind, but their view of you.

If this sounds like some sort of architectural golden rule, so be it. Particularly if you are so fortunate as to be able to afford a big waterview lot, ask not (or not only) how you can maximize your view; rather ask: How can you enhance the view of the many others for whom your house will form part of the shorescape? Hint: an ostentatious trophy house may not be the best way to celebrate and respect your trophy view.

Such decisions should never be left to designers, builders or developers. They are not the ones who will be living in the neighborhood. They simply don't have the same incentive to use design to enhance neighborly relations.

MORE SOLUTION
THAN PROBLEM

WELLFLEET RECEIVED A STIFF DOSE of design expertise a few weeks ago. Our Planning Board invited a group of students from the Harvard Graduate School of Design to come and study our town and come up with suggestions for improvement—you know, sort of take us on as a project, see if something can't be done with this underdesigned little burg. Wellfleet's Town Forum then sponsored an afternoon at which the students presented their solutions to the problems they found.

I guess if you invite eager young grad students to come and lavish their pre-professional skills on you, you have to be prepared for them to do it. Identifying problems and coming up with solutions is what they do, their reason for being.

The Harvard students noticed, for one thing, that through some oversight our town center got settled inconveniently some half mile from our harbor and that our water resources—ponds, ocean and bay beaches—were haphazardly scattered all over town when the glacier pulled out. They suggested correcting this mess by employing something called "linkage," a potent arrow in their quiver of "design concepts" they were just itching to use. Linkage seemed to have something to do with making people at point A more aware of the virtues of point B and maybe making it easier to get there.

Of course, people have been getting from Main Street to harbor, from ponds to ocean to bay for a long time using the old fashioned concept of roads, some dirt, some paved. Given the fact that people find this town attractive enough to spend ridiculous sums to be able to reside here for a week in the summer, the students might have taken a moment to ask: what is there about the inefficiency of our town layout and the roundabout ways we get around that works to make us so loveable?

The students suggested, in the words of one newspaper account, "strategies to make the Central Village more attractive." You would think, given our rep for attracting tourists and retirees and other washashores from far and wide the students would have spent their time studying exactly what there is about our village that draws and holds people. Maybe they could have discovered the recipe and written it up for use in towns more embellished with malls, gated communities and other improvements involving masterplanning and professional designing.

It's not that the students were unaffected by our charm. But they deplored how little we have done with it. You have these views, why in heaven's name don't you exploit them, point them out with signs (PICTUR-ESQUE VISTA HERE), provide view spots, like those along highways with binoculars trained on points of interest; make them more accessible to visitors.

And yet as many of us who have been here for a while seem to realize, it is no doubt the unadvertised and unexploited nature of our beauty, our relative lack of self-consciousness, that is part and parcel of our charm (compare with such exploited venues as the Hamptons and Aspen). One might have hoped that sophisticated pre-professionals would appreciate the irony that a town largely unblessed over the centuries by attention from professional designers should end up such an attractive and pleasant place to live.

Christopher Alexander, an architect who has made a career out of studying successful, charming, humanly workable dwellings and towns starts his most influential (although apparently not influential enough) book by noting that the old towns in Europe most widely admired and sought out by American tourists evolved without the help of those of his profession; indeed, the profession didn't even exist as such until not much over a 100 years ago.

Let me see, how can I say this without sounding self-satisfied, ungrateful . . . even anti-intellectual? What seems quite obvious is that we are lucky enough to live in a town that is far more solution than problem, has far more to teach than to learn. Little Outer Cape towns like this lead the nation by our backwardness. In a period of justified despairing of our culture, we offer some hope. Which is why our tourists come here.

We have here the good stuff; we are the good stuff. As the cranberry juice company that ripped off our name to push its products recognizes, we could bottle it and sell it; we do in fact every summer season, for a pretty penny.

All of which is not to say that we have no problems. But the problems we have—such as pollution and congestion due to overdevelopment, suburbanization of our rural quality of life, and the maintenance of demographic diversity—will not be solved by the approach taken by these pre-professionals. On the contrary.

Our base problem, when you come down to it, is a failure to appreciate sufficiently what we have here and how it is threatened by the amount and sort of growth and development economic, culture that plagues much of the rest of the nation. And the approach of these well-meaning, bright, and invariably polite young Harvard students—the whole arrogance of the master designer mentality—are part of that problem, not part of the solution.

POUNCE

WELLFLEET, OMNIPOINT INC'S latest conquest, will soon, thanks to the eagerness of our town officials to play ball, boast a spanking new cell phone antenna in a church steeple smack in the middle of town. It will add a whole new dimension to the meaning of that famous town landmark, home of our famous town clock.

I have come to realize that, in addition to fears I have learned to have of possible health consequences of cell technology's microwave radiation, this installation touches me deeply in another way: after a lifetime of slip slidin' away from The System, it has finally nailed me, and in a place I had come to regard above all others as a safe haven.

For me, moving to this Outer Cape town culminated a lifetime of keeping a low profile. I am not alone in this. Getting and staying Away from It All—mainstream America, suburbia, urbia, industrial parks, malls, straight corporate life, bedroom communities, the whole thing— is an essential part of our idea of ourselves, the meaning of this place.

Alternative lifeslyle doesn't begin to capture the idea.

A lifetime Thoreau fan, I believed from early on that you can march to a different drummer. All you had to do was dodge the draft (easy enough to feel OK about that with a war like Vietnam), and practice other forms of civil disobedience: live cheap, avoid a consumer need for upper-end stereos and fancy sports cars, and the corporate salaries needed to fund these fetishes.

I confess I did have a straight career for a while there, but a large part of the reason I got into English professoring was that, with its loose hours and virtuously low pay, it seemed the epitome of a low profile career—the career version of no career at all.

Of course having the good sense to be born too late for WWII and Korea and in one of the few countries left physically unscathed—the landscape at least—by the world wars helped. Arranging to be sufficiently white and neither too rich nor too poor didn't hurt either. I was blessed by birth with natural camouflage.

With all this amazing luck, I thought I had gotten off scot-free. Even though, like other products of the '60s, I talk about and believe in The System, which means, if it means anything at all, that we are all stuck in this together, that there is no escape, I confess I usually mean all except me. For me the System has been a cat crouched at the edge of my mouse existence: always dangerous, poised to pounce, but with luck it won't spot me.

I have milked the defining New World myth bigtime: this is a big old country, offering us nondescript white male types plenty of space in which to hide out—space like this little Outer Cape town, as a matter of fact.

Until recently we beyond the rotary have been too far and too sparsely populated most of the year to attract the attention of corporate suitors. We have, so far, not had to fight off the unwanted advances of the likes of Home Depot, Wal-Mart, McDonalds. We have in actual fact played wallflower at the dance of contemporary capitalism—and been pretty content with that role.

Until recently. Until the cell phone industry started to come a-courtin'. Now I feel, most painfully, tracked to my very lair.

I used to worry about the mucky grey skies of summer in Hartford, where I sojourned for many years, the air on certain days declared not fit for human consumption. (Exactly what was a breathing-type creature to do on such days?) I remember the depressing feeling of looking up into the rainy California skies when the first wave of pollution from Chinese nuclear testing hit that coast in the '60s and thinking, with the words of Joan Baez's lament, "What have they done to the rain?" They are, most obscenely, everywhere.

But I never felt as had by the Powers That Be as now by Omnipoint, which warned us in advance with that name that, by god, they would be everywhere, in our very church steeple beaming out those microwaves night and day.

What have they done to my home?

JEFFERSON'S KITCHEN
AND THE C-2 ZONE

I GREW UP IN WHAT we later learned to call a "bedroom community." All the daddies took the commuter train into The City to do whatever it was they did in there—the point was to keep us from focussing on that, even while we lived off the proceeds—and returned in the evening, having taken as many drinks on the train as needed to make the adjustment between the work front and the domestic front. This was the middle-class suburban ideal, the zenith of mid-20th century living arrangements.

My adopted hometown of Wellfleet here on the Way Outer Cape is no bedroom community. It's a matter of geography for one thing—we are too far from a city or beltway corporate zone for realistic commuting. It has just always been accepted practice, codified in zoning when that refinement came along, to allow residents to operate businesses out of their homes.

However, the bedroom community concept may be making inroads here. There is an article on the Town Meeting warrant that, if passed, would create commercial zones for purpose of taking pressure off residential neighborhoods, where there have been in recent years a growing number of complaints about unsightly or otherwise unacceptable apparatus of home-operated business. Local contractors, tradespeople and fishermen are asking for places in town to put their stuff—sacrificial zones, such as certain stretches of Route 6 or the transfer station.

At a Planning Board hearing a few weeks ago, the tradespeople present were all assurances that, in the proposed new zones, their backhoes and trucks and so on would be well shielded by fences and hedges. There was a distinctly defensive tone to their pitch—hey, we know we're ugly, we're noisy, we're objectionable. But you'll hardly know the stuff is there, they claimed.

Even as some in attendance wondered if an 800-pound gorilla could so easily be concealed, it was clear these guys were all too eager to become invisible. Apparently there is a growing tide of opinion in town which makes them feel they ought to be invisible.

I am all for tradespeople and fishermen getting some additional space if they feel they need it. What concerns me is the possibility that a sort of bedroom community aesthetic is getting a toehold in this traditional working town. One idea of what makes a town like Wellfleet attractive is a pretty, picture-postcard façade with all the nuts and bolts—all signs of what keeps it going—kept well offstage. Even one of our most traditional and appropriate businesses, shellfishing, has come under attack in recent years by owners of beachfront property who have come to view the sight of people working the flats as a blight on their view.

And yet some of the most cherished old photos of our town of early this century or late last century feature not pink roses climbing a sweet olde cottage or tourists at recreation but machinery, working oyster shacks, working boats, as well as men at work. We grow downright nostalgic over these glimpses of a self-sufficient, productive town—a town that is not just a pretty picture. So why the need to hustle their present-day counterparts out of sight?

One of our country's most celebrated houses is Monticello, the Virginia mountaintop home of Thomas Jefferson. A striking feature of this house is that the dining room where TJ and his friends met to drink wine and theorize about how to run the country was located on one floor, while hidden away in the cellar was the kitchen with its slaves producing the meal. Meals would appear as if by magic, conveyed up to the dining room by dumbwaiters. The diners wanted to see and smell and consume the product; they didn't want to be reminded of the means of production, especially given what we like to think was, for TJ at least, the embarrassment of the slave basis of his domestic life.

There is much about Monticello that appeals to me, but I must say the present-day aesthetic based on the openness of dining area to living room to kitchen and the honest featuring of the means of meal production is a vast improvement over Jefferson's segregated design.

There is something honest and vital—and even, yes, aesthetically appealing, in a way that many around here understand—about the look and feel of a town where working and living are not segregated. If the ghettoizing of the means of production gets out of hand, that would constitute a real loss.

THE ALL-TOWN
TOWN MEETING

IN JANUARY, A COMMITTEE charged with coming up with suggestions for improving Town Meeting gave a report to the Wellfleet Town Forum. As part of its work it revisited the idea of the Saturday Town Meeting. According to the committee, a number of towns in the region, including Duxbury and Fairhaven, hold Town Meeting on Saturday.

I recently read a book about Washington, New Hampshire, a much smaller town than Wellfleet, where they've always had Saturday Town Meeting. It runs all day, starting mid-morning and running as long as it takes. The author made it sound like pretty much the whole town turns out for the meeting, and that if it were ever to degenerate into a "short evening meeting attended by a tenth of the voters"—which more or less describes Wellfleet's typical meeting—it would be "time for elegies."

Wellfleet itself used to hold Town Meeting on Saturdays, according to the old-timers on the committee. When asked why that tradition was abandoned, and the meeting changed to a weekday night, they cited changes after WWII. A larger, less homogeneous population, created by the accelerating influx of washashores (retirees and other varieties), had diluted the community that formed the basis for the old-fashioned sort of Town Meeting.

Presumably the Saturday meeting was originally chosen as a non-workday when everyone was free to come. In some of the communities that have still have a Saturday meeting, daycare is provided. Of course these days a lot of people work on Saturdays so there might not be that advantage. Several hours of wrangling at Town Meeting after working all day might not be everyone's cup of tea, but at least it is theoretically possible for everyone to attend a weekday evening meeting. There is no conflict between work and civic duty.

The childcare issue is important. The best many families, with all the civic zeal in the world, can do these days is send one parent as a representative of the family while the other one stays home with the kids. That amounts to de facto disenfranchisement of half that family's legal say about town affairs, as compared with, say, a retired couple both able to attend all nights of Town Meeting.

The traditional all-day Saturday meeting is not just our Monday evening meeting (and as many subsequent evenings as needed) moved to Saturday. Judging from the description of Washington, N.H.'s meeting, the whole concept is different. Instead of the 300 or so citizens, or about one-eighth of eligible voters, we get on good night with a hot item on the warrant (that number falling off dramatically the second night), the whole town turns out. It's a townwide social event, with catered lunch and dinner if necessary. Apparently there is a bit of a festival atmosphere, with bake and craft sales.

In our town people ask their friends: "Going to Town Meeting?" as if it's an option. Sure, you know you ought to go; on the other hand, what's on TV tonight? (Good thing TM never runs as far into the week as Thursday.) In the tradition of the all-day Saturday meeting it would make about as much sense to ask if one planned to attend the nor'easter. Town Meeting day just happens. It's a civic event that, although held in one building, descends on the whole town. In a sense, the town turns into Town Meeting for that one day a year.

Some of those present at the Forum meeting where the committee made its report responded: What's all the fuss about low attendance? It accurately reflects who is interested. And what a mess if everyone showed up. Where would they all sit? We are very jaded these days about low election turnouts, about low interest in politics in general. Under fifty-percent turnout for presidential elections has been the rule for decades. Cynicism is the rule, and we all seem to accept that even if we ourselves choose to participate. Learning of the way it used to be here and the way it still is in some other towns provides interesting perspective on our low expectations.

Perhaps it was inevitable, as the committee members seemed to suggest, that changes in the demographic composition and size of our town killed off the old all-day Saturday Town Meeting. Maybe its death was an expression of our decline and fall from the glory days when our town was a real town. On the other hand, maybe the re-institution of the tradition—not just the different day but the whole different concept—could begin to reverse the trend of our cynicism, our alienation from even this small town government.

THE ABSORBABILITY
THEME

HERE IN WELLFLEET, we have yet another instance of what we could call the Absorbability Theme.

The state Department of Environmental Protection is leaning on the town to create a public water supply. It says the nitrate levels in the private wells downtown indicate that the time has come to abandon the traditional way of getting water: dig a hole where you need it and pump it up.

Seems like this Absorbability Theme keeps popping up these days. When we switched not so many years ago from a dump to a transfer station, we were admitting that the land our town sits on could no longer absorb all the garbage and junk we might want to dump there. Now we park it in a big container, which gets trucked to someone else's backyard over the bridge.

Our existing highway can no longer absorb all the traffic that tries to get down it in the summer. People talk about widening the road to make room for all the nice people who want to favor us with a visit in the summer.

We are about to vote in town meeting to create a commercial zone to absorb the overflow of business activity that can no longer, some say, be absorbed in the traditional way by the neighborhoods where the tradesmen and fisherman live.

Now it turns out that the land our town sits on can no longer absorb the septage produced by our households and businesses. The remedy would be to tap water supplies in a reserve wellfield in the National Seashore a couple of miles away.

Unlike the citizens of highly developed urban and suburban areas who are often oblivious to the source of such a basic necessity as drinking water, in this small town we have an intimate relationship with our water because it comes from under our feet. We know where the well is and where the septic system is; we know that whatever escapes the latter goes into the same ground that is the source of the water we drink. For many, knowing the sand under one's feet is sufficiently absorptive to make our homesteads self-sustaining is one of the basic pleasures of living here.

When I lived in a small inland city, I got a kick out of not bagging my leaves every fall and leaving them along the street to be hauled elsewhere by the city. I liked avoiding the nuisance of packing leaves in bags. I liked avoiding the cost of buying the bags. But most of all, I took real pleasure in knowing that my city lot could absorb those leaves when I just heaped them, along with the hedge prunings, on my back lot line. I liked to think of it as the Self-Composting Yard.

I am very fond of the fact that my acre of Wellfleet woods has so far been able to compost the leaves that fall from the trees as well as the effluent from our septic system.

Some people, stressed out by summer traffic on Route 6, say, "Wow, look at all the cars. Let's make an Outer Cape interstate for them and greater numbers to follow." Others, though, react differently: "Wow, isn't there some way we can reduce the numbers of people trying to crowd into our towns?" To many in this town, the story about high nitrates in downtown wells is not a signal to borrow water from across town, rob Peter to pay

Paul, because we happen to be lucky enough to have an area of forced underdevelopment from which to borrow. Rather, it is a hint that, as predicted by the Cape Cod Commission's "Outer Cape Capacity Study" of 1996, the development chickens are coming home to roost. Not expansion but limits should be our watchword.

Solving our nitrate problem by borrowing water from across town would be tantamount to suppressing a symptom—not a good idea if you want to cure the disease.

OBLIVIOUSNESS
OF THINGS PAST

WITNESSING THE CHANGE in the Commercial
Street lineup brought about by the demolishing of the old
police and fire station gets me thinking about all the
changes I've seen in my time as tourist and resident
here—but even more about the changes that, although
they happened during my time, I for some reason did not
notice. The recently demolished building, for instance:
although it makes a certain amount of difference in its
absence, I have little or no memory of noticing it when it
was there, although we co-existed for a lot of years. In
fact, it first got my attention as a literary reference, as the
major setting for Alec Wilkinson's book about his mid-
'70s experience as a Wellfleet cop, *Midnights*. I remember
thinking, when I read that book in the early '80s: wow,
imagine all that going on in a building that was to me, at
that very same time, little more than a blur as I walked by.

What do tourists know? Like a lot of part-time
romancers of this town, I paid more attention to ocean
and ponds in those days than features of town life. But
when it comes to not noticing things, my obliviousness of
the old police and fire station is small potatoes compared
with the astounding failure of my powers of observation
vis a vis the town pier. According to Judy Stetson's
Wellfleet: A Pictorial History, when I first visited here, in

September 1959, the pier, the 600-space parking lot which became the dominant feature of the harbor, was still under construction. How could one not notice such a monstrosity? Wouldn't the smell of the tar from the blacktopping of the surface have still been competing obnoxiously with the salt air? But, of course, I never knew Shirttail Point, the sandbar entombed in the pier, and so in a sense could not have known, even assuming my eyes took in the scene, the full meaning of the crime being perpetrated.

The very year of that first visit, an impressive mansard roof mansion at the corner of Main and Holbrook, the Wellfleet Hotel in its final avatar, was torn down in favor of the undistinguished low-sloped-roofed brick building that became the controversial post office (controversial when a developer succeeded in having the service moved to Route 6 despite considerable protest against removing an important function of the traditional downtown). Ruth Rickmers, author of the *Wellfleet Remembered: Past to Present in Pictures* series, remembers that the Wellfleet Hotel was torn down because it was considered too needy of repair. It must have been painful for anyone who knew it to see what replaced it. I wonder: just when in that year was it demolished? Is it possible I saw it? And if I did, why didn't I register dismay when, on my next visit, there was the diminished offspring?

Stetson writes: "The same year that the marina was completed the last train passed through Wellfleet." That would be 1960. The railroad still operating in this town in my time? Amazing. According to Stetson, the passenger service had been discontinued in the '30s, and the freight depot demolished in 1953. Apparently the trains kept coming only to serve the railroad itself by carrying sand from Provincetown for use in train brakes, and when they started doing that by truck there was no more need for a train out here. So, it was a mere shadow of its former self during that first visit of mine, but still, an experience of another era . . .had I actually experienced it. As it was, another historical watershed of which I was oblivious.

The first Wellfleet Town Hall I ever saw—must have seen, although, again, I don't   remember—was the original, the one that had been moved to Main Street earlier in the century from South Wellfleet. I learned this only years later by reading the local historians. In March 1960, several months after my first visit, I was sliding on dining hall trays with friends down a hill in Providence in a wild blizzard while at the very same time, unknown to me, Town Hall was burning to the ground. The next time I returned, June of that year, you would think there must have been a really obvious lack of Town Hall dominating Main Street—perhaps some foundation, some charred remains, the unharmed vault that, I'm told, remained in use when town offices took temporary refuge in the Elementary School. But did I notice one way or the other? Nope. What do tourists know? At some point, of course, I remember being aware there was a Town Hall— there had to have been because we played Frisbee on its lawn, precursors of today's hackey-sackers. At some point I read it was only a replica of the original.

One of the biggest features of town when I first visited was lack of a National Seashore park, and once again I experienced, while failing to notice, that absence. On my first visit and then again the following summer I slept several nights on the ocean beach. Had I known anything at all about the real life of the town beyond my little romance with the beaches and the surface charm, I would have known that a huge controversy was raging over the looming advent of the Seashore. Had I known that, those nights on the beach would have had a whole other meaning; I could have savored the last moments of that era of unregulated freedom.

But what do tourists know?

OASIS, SPEEDBUMP,
GUERILLA BASE

I USED TO THINK radical politics was an urban thing—sit-ins and demonstrations at Berkeley, Columbia, Cambridge, marches on Washington, organizing in the inner city. But these days just trying to stay a small, rural town is a radical act.

We don't have to go somewhere else to sit-in, just sit in on planning board hearings on cell phone antenna sitings. We don't have to take a bus to Washington to demonstrate, just demonstrate some spunk as citizens in our own town. All we have to do—all we can do, really—is fight the good fight in behalf of what we believe. Those beliefs are not the abstract, peace 'n love ideals of the '60s, but the down-to-earth values inherent in this place: our small size, localness, community, the right to enjoy the space around us, to run our local businesses. All the things that make a little town like ours what it is.

Time was when the small town was the basic unit of American capitalism. Citizens of a town like Wellfleet were just honest folks trying to get ahead, run their businesses. "What's good for General Motors is good for the U.S.A." (as the president of that company infamously said back in the '50s) got no argument from most small-town citizens. There was no contradiction, it seemed at any rate, between the life of a small town and capitalism at its most powerful levels. We even had our famous local capitalist success in Lorenzo Dow Baker, the banana king, founder of United Fruit. (Capitalism feels different when you export it than when it is trying to shoehorn its way into your life.)

Quite clearly that is no longer the case. Now for the first time the life of our town has come to seem a contradiction with the American Way of Life, or at least the corporate part of it that has come to seem so dominant.

The most obvious example is the cellular phone industry's assault on the Cape. In town after town, this one among them, hearings have been packed with those who oppose becoming part of the grid cell phone companies are imposing on the globe—or at least the industry's insensitivity to local concerns over health, aesthetics and property values.

The cell phone assault is not the only one. Until recently it has always seemed that we of the Outer Cape were too small a year-round market too far off the beaten path to attract the attention of bigtime corporations such as MacDonalds or Home Depot. Now, as our fulltime population creeps up, with franchises and chains establishing beachheads up-Cape, a common attitude is that it is only a matter of time before we too become globalized.

To get our thinking straight, our town, like others, has spent many citizen hours coming up with a Comprehensive Plan spelling out in great detail what we care about here, what our quality of life consists of—both the natural environment and the life of the community— and a strategy for ensuring its survival on into the future. Just browse through our Plan and you soon see that it is a radical document, in that it recognizes that there is a fundamental contradiction between big national and international capitalism (malls, chains, franchises) and such innocent-seeming values as localness and smallness.

The Local Comprehensive Plan is a Declaration of Independence of sorts.

Preserving our quality-of-life has an interesting effect of making strange bedfellows of erstwhile Republicans and Democrats, progressives and conservatives. The usual nomenclature gets scrambled. Progressives get to calling themselves conservationists, if not conservatives, wanting to conserve both the local animal species and the most endangered species of all, small-town life. Retirees who may have spent most of their lives working for a suburban corporation and feeling quite comfortable with pro-business government, for the first time find themselves at the receiving end of corporate aggression and see the negative effects on the town they have chosen. Those on the right support the socialist wing of the U.S. government, our National Park, when it conflicts with private property rights.

From the point of view of mega-corporate forces of globalization sweeping the post-cold war world a small town like ours is clearly anathema, a speedbump. (You can hear it in the tone of the agents of progress sent here by the cell phone companies: This is the way things are going, people, don't you get it? Get outta the way.)

From our grassroots point of view we are an oasis, an enclave. A guerilla base.

PEOPLE CHOWDER

THE POND BEGINS TO SOUND different at some point in the late summer. The high-pitched scree-ing sounds at times like the little creatures—insects? frogs?—steeping themselves in the last warmth of summer, a sound of deep peace. Sometimes it seems a tentative, plaintive note that anticipates the storms of winter.

This year, it sounds like the pond breathing a sigh of relief.

All outrageous anthropomorphism, of course; but it has been a tough summer at the pond. Even back in spring the water level was way down, and this after very high levels for the past two years which flooded all the little beaches where people like to spread their blankets. Those of us with nothing better to do than worry about such things worried: what if we get another dry winter and a correspondingly big drop from these low levels?

All summer the water level has continued to drop and, with all that exposed beach, it seems there have been more people than ever trying to get at it. With all the families enjoying the pond, the slathering of suntan lotion, the kids in diapers happily splashing in the shallows and other features of the idyllic family scene, it has been hard to avoid those inner calculations of the ratio of sweat, lotion and urine to H2O.

Part of it is the water temperature. This was a hot summer and by early July the ponds felt tepid, like a heated pool. The chemistry major in all of us senses that turning up the Bunsen burner can only produce a richer, more potent stew of pollutants. I know a number of local parents who would think themselves derelict in their duty for allowing their kids to swim in the ponds in season. One family installed one of those plastic above-ground pools—the sort of thing Cape Codders associate with the poor, deprived life of the landlocked 'burbs—and kept their kids confined to it all summer long rather than risk pollution by tourists at the several ponds within easy walking distance.

Test results duly posted by John Chatham, our health agent, show the levels of pollutants well within the government's safe range. John says the summertime use doesn't actually do the polluting that one intuitively feels it does. Still, official postings notwithstanding, a note of desperation has been part of the atmosphere of the ponds.

Last month, the Wellfleet Forum held a meeting of summer residents and they got going with horror stories about the ponds. One guy talked about parents (tourists, naturally) actually stripping the diapers from their toddlers and encouraging them to express themselves fecally in the water, right in amongst the throng of fellow pond-goers. There were stories of dogs in the water, against Seashore regs, about people washing with soap.

Even while painting this unsavory picture, which you would think would send sensible people scurrying, holding their noses, back to those chlorinated backyard pools, many of these part-timers complained bitterly about being deprived of their customary access to ponds. "Used to be you could spend the afternoon there . . . Now arrive at 3 and if you're lucky you get to stand in line with your engine running waiting for a parking space to open up."

The whole feeling of this meeting was of peoples' entitlement: I'll be damned if that pond isn't going to give me what I WANT. I WILL have my piece of primetime at the pond, I will, I will. There was talk of enlarging parking lots, of running shuttle busses out there. Sounded to me like working a loyal servant to death.

Any longtime pond aficionado can remember 15 or 20 years ago when you could lie around at some of the more out-of-the-way ponds all day long in so much seclusion it seemed perfectly natural to have your clothes off much of the time. I never used to feel that I had to plan my visits around the crowds; I could have the pond to myself just about anytime of the day. Now, it's shorter hits earlier and later. It's not quite the relaxed situation of yesteryear. I have to be more strategic, more realistic. I can't have as much of it as I used to. The pond doesn't have it to give.

We've had several rains; the temperatures have begun to drop, making the pond less liable to comparison with bacterial chowder. With (I swear) a sigh of relief, it heads into a long winter of recovery mode. Maybe next summer the water levels will once again keep down the number of pond-lovers crowding the margins.

THE BIG AND THE SMALL

IN ONE WIDELY HELD VIEW, progress in human civilization is the history of smaller social and political units becoming bigger ones. Clans become tribes become principalities. The fiefdoms of Middle-Aged England, France, Germany or Italy are transcended to yield the modern nations.

Of course, the late, unlamented Soviet Union, which might be thought of as one culmination of this process, seemed to show the limits of monolithism. With its breakup into its constituent parts 10 years ago, suddenly small units were all the rage. Then again, the celebrating over the reversion to smallness and diversity in the FSU and Yugoslavia has been severely dampened by the failure of the re-emerged small units to celebrate each other.

In short, the jury is out on whether big units or small units work best.

Around here, "regionalization" often applies to schools, and again the prevailing opinion has been that the movement on the Outer Cape from individual town schools to the Nauset region has been a good and necessary thing. There has been, as far as I know, little official second-guessing of that decision to regionalize back in the late '50s. On the other hand, a constant theme among a lot of elementary school parents during my son's time there (he is now a 7th grader) was regret at having to send our kids to the larger unit. There was the daily one-and-a-half to two-hour commute, one unavoidable drawback of going nonlocal. But beyond that, a hunch— perhaps just a romantic prejudice—that our kids would be better off if we could keep them close by for another couple of years, that a certain amount of the usual dread of middle school was avoidable if we didn't have to submit our kids to the region.

Regionalization of our schools had been going on long before the creation of the Nauset region over 40 years ago. Consolidation of the neighborhoods within Wellfleet itself was the original regionalization. Until not much more than 100 years ago, reflecting the then far-flung neighborhoods of which our town consisted, education in this town was conducted in a dozen or so one-room schools scattered all over town. Gradually, as the ascendency of the present town center grew, these small neighborhood schools consolidated into fewer, larger buildings. Regionalization within Wellfleet took a final step when the original portion of the present elementary school was constructed in 1938 to house K-12. Finally, in 1956, the town made the rather momentous decision that the larger region could look after its children's education better than the town itself.

I am told that the main argument that led to regionalization in the first place, and that still holds sway with many who might otherwise have a sentimental attachment to staying local, is financial. Sure, staying local might be nice and who really wants their kids to be spending all that time on the bus? But the regional school can offer so much more—physical plant, programs, extracurricular activities, sport facilities, and so on. But I wonder how much of that list is at the heart and soul of education? Letting that argument about the limits of parochialism run, small towns have less in general to offer than cities and suburbs. But many in this town think the small unit, at least this town's small unit, has certain advantages over the larger units of suburb and urb. If big units are clearly superior, why is the Lighthouse School widely regarded as a great success and an implicit critique of many aspects of the Middle School?

It would seem an expression of faith of a town in itself to see its influence on its own children as positive—to want to have a longer rather than a shorter influence. Campus Wellfleet has much to recommend it in the way of visible history, creative citizens, a variety of traditional occupations (as well as a library, computers, travel and other links to the great world).

There are now 50 to 75 fewer kids at Wellfleet Elementary than when my son started in '92. Wouldn't that make enough room to keep 6th grade here, at the very least? And perhaps the 7th and 8th grades as well? Let's re-think regionalization.

ALL GAME, NO SIDELINES

WARNING TO CONSUMERS: what follows is not an open-minded, evenhanded, objective column. It contains a point of view. The author, a citizen of the town in which and of which he writes, is an Interested Party; that is, he drinks the water from the ground about whose quality public debate now rages. He has a child in the school system, makes money from tourists, is subject to whatever effects might result from long range exposure to microwave antennas the town pleases to allow cell phone companies to install. He has served on town boards and committees and spoken up at public hearings. He is, in short, like every citizen, an actor in the very unfolding history of which he writes. Indeed it is the whole purpose of this column (as quixotic as it may sound) to have an effect on the course of that history by influencing the thinking of readers.

Over the past year or so Wellfleet's Board of Selectmen made numerous appointments to the planning board, part of whose important work is to regulate cell phone antenna placement. Some of the candidates for positions had publically urged caution in siting antennas because of possible health consequences reported by some studies. None of the candidates with such an agenda were appointed.

The board viewed all those candidates as disqualified in having a bias in this important issue facing the town. The board's appointees included a man who had, in a speech in town meeting, declared all those citizens comprising the strong majority who had voted the cautious position of not locating a tower near our school "silly" for their concerns; and another man who was the main spokesman for the Congregational Church in its efforts to make money by leasing its tower to a cell phone company.

The selectmen, inclined to trust federal and corporate reassurances about such things as public health (several of the selectmen themselves were retirees from executive positions in government and corporations, one from Raytheon, the leader in microwave technology), clearly stacked the planning board with people who would vote to ease cell phone companies into town with a minimum of fuss and bother.

Did the board see itself as biased in its actions, as nakedly exercising power against the clear will of the people as expressed in town meeting votes? I doubt it. I imagine the board saw itself as protecting the town against anti-cell phone zealots and appointing levelheaded, mature citizens not caught up in the silly health panic. One set of candidates were seen as having an axe to grind, the other as wielding nothing so threatening. The anti-position was defined as a position, the pro- as no position at all.

The exercise of power by this board was facilitated by the widespread misconception that there is in fact such a thing as disinterested, serenely open-minded citizens without axes to grind—citizens who, while caring a great deal are somehow less a part of things than others.

It is true that open-mindedness in the sense of "willing to learn" is a virtue. But disinterestedness in citizenship—sometimes it masquerades as its first cousin, professional administrative competence—is a red herring, more often than not.

Those who live in large, impersonal suburbs or cities can be forgiven for feeling that there is lots of neutral, unpolitical space. There are the politicians, the movers and shakers, the ones running for or holding office, the ones making all the noise and headlines; and then there are the rest of us, the ones moved and shaken, the ones that politics are done to. You are unlikely to know the movers and shakers who make the decisions that shape your life.

In a little town like Wellfleet, however, you are very likely to know who is voting this way or that, on an antenna siting proposed for your neighborhood, on the survival of a favorite restaurant, on whether you can add that extra bedroom. If in the big world it's six degrees of separation in a town like this it's more like one or two. If we are not on a board ourselves, we are very likely to know someone who is, someone whose vote can be influenced by conversation over coffee.

Here is it clear that everyone has an axe to grind, which is not to say that we are more narrowminded, stubborn, opinionated, meaner in our politics than citizens of other towns, but only that in this context it is easy to see that we are all part of the fabric of this town. We all have a stake in what we all do. As I think Eldridge Cleaver was trying to say in his famous slogan about being part of the problem or part of the solution, everything is political; it's all game, no sidelines.

BEING A
HOT COMMODITY

IT IS FRONT PAGE NEWS now that, among the other radically disturbing changes in life on Olde Cape Cod, some of us can't afford to live here any more. It's getting to where the average Cape Cod house and the average Cape Cod family, belonging to different socioeconomic classes, are no longer on speaking terms.

There's a twist to this predicament of Cape Codders not being able to afford to rent or buy on Cape Cod: Cape Codders who do own houses and can't afford to live in them. At least during the summer season, these homeowners find the tourist rental money irresistible.

I don't know just when I first heard that paradoxical sounding assertion, "I can't afford to live in my own house," but it wasn't until the '80s real estate boom that it occurred to me that it might apply to me. We owned a handyman's special in a small city, paying only $148 a month in mortgage payments, affordable housing even on a meager academic salary. My wife and I occupied most of the house and rented out a small apartment for all of $75 or $100 a month, as much for company in this big, old haunted house as for the money.

Then came the boom. For the first time, my affordable housing took on the added dimension of commodity.

I mentioned it to my wife: "You know, this apartment (our part of the house, a spacious three bedrooms) is probably worth 700-800 bucks a month now. I'm starting to feel like those people who say they can't afford to live in their own house. Since when could we afford a luxury $800 apartment?" Suddenly it felt as if we were paying that big rent because that was the money we were doing ourselves out of by choosing to take up that much space. My wife, never one to mince her words, said, "I hate that way of thinking. I can't live like that."

I had always hated that way of thinking too. I guess it is one of those things we resist, especially those of us not particularly well positioned in the money game: the idea of everything and everyone having a price tag. We hated that way of thinking, but before long we had moved to the small attic apartment in that house to be able to take advantage of the rent we could get on the more luxurious one downstairs we had been calling home.

Now here it is, different boom, different place but we find ourselves caught up in a variation on the same economic theme: the summer rents are so good we can't afford to live in our house. We used to rent casually, often to friends, for more or less what we ourselves could afford to pay for a vacation rental. But our summer renters these days pay much more than we or almost anyone else we know can imagine shelling out for a week of a roof over our head.

We engage in giddy bull market gossip with friends doing the same thing: "I can't believe what we're getting this summer. Can you imagine paying $1500, $1800, $2000 a week?" "Did you hear this one family paid $20,000 for a month for a waterfront place? Can you imagine? That's a downpayment." The rents seem embarrassing, ridiculous, crazy. We also know that this attitude says more about our impoverished imaginations than about the reality of two salary families living in the suburbs. When they wave the money at us, we move out.

We are comforted somewhat by knowing that the same temptation is being succumbed to all over town: people moving out and leaving for a vacation they really didn't know they needed or even wanted, crashing with relatives, several families banding together to rent a large, rundown house (unsuitable for summer people) for the season, people camping out in a modified garage or barn.

Until now we have always drawn the line at renting out of season. September is time to reassert family stability, get our son settled back into his room in time for school. But this year we succumbed. Someone saw our ad on the Internet, made us an offer we couldn't refuse for a week in mid-September. We were all set to take the money and move back to our cramped summer quarters when the deal fell through. But we had taken another step in the commodification of our house, of our lives.

Who makes enough money, we wonder, that they can resist $1500 when all you have to do is leave your house for a week? Everyone has a price, right? An economist could probably calculate the exact income level at which that kind of rent becomes resistible. It is above ours.

And yes, of course, as we do frequently remind ourselves, those of us who bought before the boom, aren't we lucky we have a hot commodity to peddle? Those who can't afford a house at all should just have our problem.

TO HANG
OR NOT TO HANG

THE LATEST CHALLENGE to my already shaky romance with this town is learning in recent weeks that there is a longstanding controversy about whether to let kids, when they reach a certain age, hang out in downtown Wellfleet.

Turns out a significant portion of parents regard our innocent looking, charming downtown, focused on the lawn of that bastion of our civic life, our Town Hall, as a den of iniquity likely to influence youth in the direction of drugs, sex, and slacker behavior. The way some people go on about the perils of downtown you would think they are talking about Times Square before Disney purged it of sleaze. Other parents, though, feel OK about it: Hey, the whole point is this is not Times Square. That's why we moved here, so our kids can safely hang out in public.

I must confess, as one who wants badly to believe in the essential virtue of this town, I have always seen downtown as more or less an extension of my own living room. When my son, now pushing 13, reached the age a couple of years ago of wanting to bike to town to see friends I was concerned with the safety of the trip there on our narrow roads, but it never occurred to me that being there was a problem with his wanting to occupy civic space.

On the contrary: How great he wants to embrace the downtown scene. There are so many places urban and suburban in the world we have left behind, where you would not feel OK about entrusting your child to the public space. But here, precisely because the patch of Town Hall lawn is in the middle of things within easy eyeshot of Main Street merchants, Town Hall workers and other passersby, many of whom know our son, what could be safer? The grapevine would work to get word back to you if something were amiss. Isn't this is precisely how community should work? If it takes a village, well then, by golly, he's got one.

It is precisely because downtown is the focus of community—for grownups as well as kids—that kids want to spend time there. This is the epicenter of town life, where it's at, the scene. We cherish the old photos of town geezers hanging out on a bench downtown chewing the fat. It seems the essence of traditional village life. Those same guys sitting in someone's living room just wouldn't be the same thing. It seems like the kids' urge to hang downtown comes from much the same civic impulse. There is another issue: When I was a kid in the suburbs all I had to do to find companions for play was walk out the door and there was an instant game of kick-the-can or Red Rover. For a kid living in a typical sparsely populated Wellfleet neighborhood, downtown is his neighborhood, the only place he can find even a small collection of peers.

America in general has turned in the second half of this century from public space to private. Older houses were all built with porches where you could sit and watch the world go by. At some point we abandoned the porch, turned away from the street, focused outdoor activity on the backyard, with or without the new equivalent of the porch, a deck. In France and Italy, among other places, an essential part of life remains civic space, a place where friends and neighbors of all ages go to hang out in outdoor cafes, play boules or dominoes, to see and be seen.

So why does it seem that for many in our town the best downtown is one looking as if the Pied Piper had just come through town? Instead of expecting our police to make sure kids are neither seen nor heard downtown we would do better to concentrate our efforts on making sure civic space remains a desirable place for all our citizens to hang out.

If in a town like this, where many feel free to leave house and car doors unlocked, the public space is not an extension of the community and home, where can it be?

HOLES IN A TOWN'S SOUL

THIS PAST SUMMER when Wellfleet's economy revved up, there were two conspicuous dead spots in the familiar Main Street lineup of businesses: West Main Books down near the library and the News Dealer right smack in the middle of things. The familiar facades are like a root canal tooth—dead, eviscerated, but still part of the smile. You could still make a postcard of our picturesque little downtown and nothing would seem amiss. (We are so long accustomed to the gaptooth effect created by the candy store fire over 20 years ago it hardly registers.)

The demolition just before summer of the old police and fire station building on Commercial Street, a longterm fixture, sets up a fear for these newly empty buildings. Will they be the next to go? Worse, what entrepreneurial opportunists will be eyeing those weak spots in the traditional fabric of our town, thinking of injecting new life into them with a McDonald's or Starbucks?

More recently, the Catholic church, another familiar presence on Main Street, announced plans to move out to the highway and to eliminate all evidence of its downtown history by razing the church. (Can you just do that, tear down a church? Isn't a church more than just studs and plywood, blessed with eternal, inviolable Significance?

Won't it be like the movie *Poltergeist,* the holy ghosts raising a ruckus?)

Scary how dependent we are on old buildings, some of them quite worn down (and yes, the decay is part of the look, part of the charm), and on traditional businesses, some of them pretty tired, too. How fragile this collection of buildings and people we call a town, this atmosphere, character, flavor, the suchness (to get Zen about it) of this exact place.

We like to say that a town is its people, and some worry that when working people, artists, old hippies and other traditional constituencies can no longer afford to live here and are replaced by retirees from the surburbs, we won't be us anymore. But in another sense, our village consists of nothing but a certain number of buildings of a certain age, all of them wearing out slowly. When they are all gone the way of the old police and fire station, will our town be gone?

There is the analogy with human cells. I've read somewhere that all our cells get replaced every so often, but we maintain continuity as an organism. Is that the way it is with the organism of a town? How about the analogy of organ and limb transplants? We are well into the era of these surgical miracles, yet doubts linger. There was that movie about the disturbing results of giving a pianist the hand of a murderer. To what extent is a person with a new heart the same person? What about when we learn brain transplants? Can a building or business transplant change the essence of a town?

When the choice is to respect the old building and put it to new uses, as in the case of the elegant new card shop on Bank Street, or a big old Main Street residence turned into a warren of shops a few years ago, do we applaud the rejuvenation, or shudder at the invasion of the body-snatchers? Aspen, Colorado still looks the old mountain and mining town, but how much of Aspen is there left after the invasion of the monied Los Angelenos? Seems to me that the look has little more meaning than a Hollywood backlot set.

Study the pictorial histories of Ruth Rickmers and Judy Stetson and you get an idea of how many impressive old buildings have been torn down or have burned down, often to be replaced by less noble—or less soulful— structures. Chequesset Hotel on Mayo Beach vs. a trailer park. The oyster shacks vs. a condo cluster. Belvernon, a dignified house on Route 6 vs. a gas station. We may employ more architects now than ever before, real estate may be booming, but it is clear that we have seen better days architecturally.

I suppose our unwavering popularity with summer visitors should give us confidence that we can't be uncharming no matter how hard we try. We apparently survived the 1959 degeneration of the mansard roofed Wellfleet Hotel into the one-story brick building that housed our former post office. We even seem to be surviving the much deplored architectural folly of the "new" P.O. on Route 6 (even worse than its undistinguished predecessor because an architect actually designed it that way). Still, when a venerable business in a prominent place goes dead, we worry. Another little piece of our town up for grabs.

GO PLAY IN THE STREET

SOMETIMES LIFE ARRANGES things so neatly for us columnists. At Wellfleet's recent special Town Meeting attention was focussed for a while on a local bylaw against skateboarding, skating, and other forms of slow, playful transportation on Main Street and other streets of our Central District. Citizens were asked (and declined, but only by a narrow margin) to put more teeth in this bylaw by increasing the fines.

The very next morning in the front section of this newspaper there was a nice big photo of a kid skateboarding down the Main Street of Cotuit. It was one of those pictures with no other purpose than illustrating the wonderful quality of life on Cape Cod. The caption read: "He had no particular destination and was just enjoying the pleasant day."

Indeed. It is an attractive image, a kid out on a nice day enjoying his town.

But that kid better not try it in Wellfleet. Such behavior could get him fined for violation of our anti-play -in -the- streets ordinance, which reads as follows: "No person shall coast, roller skate, scooter, play ball, skateboard or engage in any other athletic game on Holbrook Ave., Commercial and East Main Street or streets or public parking lots of the Central District . . ."

Until the town meeting debate called my attention to the bylaw I had always assumed that this rural town fully embraced the spirit of the newspaper photo. I had not realized we were so down on playing in the streets. (Yeah, I know, Cotuit may have its own anti-play bylaw; for all I know that kid may be languishing in juvenile hall, an unintended victim of a free-spirited photographer.)

It is a fact that a kid on a skateboard cruising down the road—or an inline skater or bicyclist of any age (our own police chief cuts quite a figure as he bikes around town)—can be an annoyance to those in cars, forcing us to exercise patience and slow down. The law implies that autos should not be so annoyed, should not burdened with the responsibility of having to watch out for vulnerable fellow human beings, but rather should be able to roll unimpeded down the streets, kings of the road.

The job of our police apparently is to enable this auto entitlement: clear the streets of all this frivolous playing so the streets can be devoted to the serious, straight-ahead business of autos getting from point A to point B. The streets belong to the cars.

It's not necessarily so. There are towns where they post SHARE THE ROAD signs. Our own town for a couple of years has a sign at the exits off Route 6 pointing out the obvious: CAUTION: NARROW STREETS. WALKERS, JOGGERS, CHILDREN. PLEASE DRIVE GENTLY.

We have those signs, but our bylaw and the emphasis of law enforcement evidently remain unclear on the concept. We need a fundamental shift to the share-the-road attitude.

Wait a minute, someone will say, isn't the main reason for keeping kids off the streets to protect them from cars? What's wrong with that? Cars are dangerous. But that's like enacting a town curfew that says people are not allowed out on the streets after dark because there are rapists and murderers out there--it's for their own good.

Not so many years ago there were numerous feminist-led Take Back the Night demonstrations to dramatize exactly that problem, that our whole societal orientation had the effect of punishing the victims, keeping women off the streets at night. Take Back the Night—Take Back the Streets. Yes, cars are dangerous, but a lot less so when going three miles per hour.

I am told that the standard way of establishing the speed limit for a section of road is to observe cars travelling that stretch with no limits and set the legal speed at the 85th percentile. (Why, I wonder, are the fastest drivers, probably the most impatient, taken as the standard? Why not, at the very least, the 50th percentile? Go ask the state, which establishes the procedure. It's a very auto-centric method in any case.) How about taking the average speed of skateboarders—or joggers—and making that the legal speed limit, at least on those roads that get a lot of non-automotive use?

An attractive, healthy downtown is a place where people—of all ages—naturally wish to congregate, to see and be seen, to hang out, to play. Let drivers be instructed: WATCH OUT FOR PEOPLE AT PLAY. A downtown enjoyable for people not in autos will and ought to be an inconvenient downtown for those in autos.

MARGINAL AMERICA

IF THERE IS ANYTHING to the American claim to being "the land of the free" it has less to do with its economic system—capitalism—which is often very regimented and oppressive than with the possibility of dropping out of it. The real America is in the cracks in the system, the nooks and crannies; not in the mainstream but the eddies and backwaters.

Some of our most characteristic heroes are not the famous generals and heads of state and captains of industry but marginal types like Pete Seeger, Woody Guthrie, John Brown, Mother Jones, Thoreau, Whitman—cutups, hermits, cranks. Thorns in the side of the body politic. Our most characteristic citizens are not the buttoned down corporate types from the suburbs but prospectors, hobos and dropouts, the cowboys our mothers are supposed to not let us grow up to be. More colorful and in some ways more consistent with American democracy than its legit capitalist sea captains are its pirates.

Speaking of which, Wellfleet has a pirate: Brian Ramsdell, known as the pirate to himself and the kids in town. 52 years old, old enough to know better, he doesn't have the usual real estate credentials for being a legit part of this town: a paid-up rental, a mortgage. "I love living on the water," he says. "I love living free. It's the most satisfying thing in the whole world." Until a storm recently trashed it, he lived on a sort of pirate ship houseboat, first cousin to the Flying Neutrinos' world circumnagivating floating trash pile.

Now Wellfleet itself is a marginal town, a town of dropouts, castoffs, artists and other spinoffs from mainstream society. But even in marginal Wellfleet there is the more and the less marginal. The marginal can be controversial; the dropped out are not always welcome. The best pizza in town over the last decade is bootleg pizza, driven underground. The margins of our harbor are littered with old boat hulls and engine blocks, none properly licensed to decay in those spots. Half the kids in town are skateboard outlaws. Our marginal theater— marginal in the sense of cutting edge— not only features naked people in its nasty, subversive plays but flushes its toilets with suspect water.

And our one pirate is under pressure from the police to strike his skull and crossbones and move along, cleanup his act. His piratical houseboat was, it turns out, moored in the wrong water and in any case was trashed in the storm. Now he sleeps in a van worrisomely tattooed with slogans: "Love stinks," "Live free," "Viagra power." More colorful than your average van. The van is presumably licensed, but he doesn't have a license to park it where he does down at the town pier.

The police and town officials want him to move along. Seems like they feel he's trying to get away with something with this "living free" business. Sure, he's a native, which usually counts for something; a minor tourist attraction and photo op and sort of a hero to our kids and, as pirates go, not much of a threat to the social order. But hell, laws are laws and what if everybody tried to live free?

Contradictions, contradictions. Yes, even a marginal town with more than its share of ancient hippies and dropouts has its laws and if you have 'em I guess you got to enforce 'em. Who would be the one to say: let everyone sleep anywhere they want in a van, in a houseboat? (What if everyone actually did it? What then? And yet how likely is that? Most prefer the comforts of a real bed).

Laws are laws and the police have a job to do, sure. And yet it seems wrong somehow that we go to great extremes protecting the endangered turtles that wash up on our beaches every winter while our response to this endangered human marine species, our one latter-day pirate, is to do our best to wipe it out.

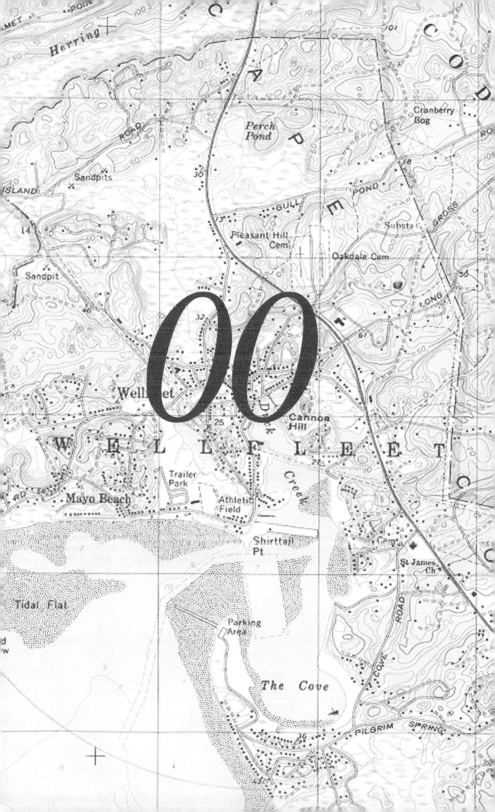

SLEEPING DOG

WELL, IT'S OFFICIAL: Wellfleet has a water problem. How do we know we have a water problem? Because the state says we do. Furthermore, we now have we have a state-sponsored solution, a no-interest 8 million dollar loan the state says would probably be available to us if we jump right on it.

The citizens of Wellfleet are being asked at an unusual, hibernation-disrupting special town meeting on Jan. 31 to vote an emergency 80 thou just to study the problem in preparation for applying for the big bucks. (One selectman calls it a virtual "downpayment"). If we vote yes on that then we will really know we've got a problem. You don't spend that kind of money without there being a big problem, right?

Well, actually...

There is a basic issue here underlying the recent and ongoing crisis over Wellfleet's downtown water situation. When is a problem a problem? Who gets to determine what constitutes a problem?

The commonsense answer: You know you have a problem when the people suffering—inconvenienced, hurt, sickened—tell you so. From their moaning and groaning and their gripes you get the idea that something should be done.

But in this case, the state has been doing almost all of the moaning and groaning, as if they are suffering from our water. But they don't live here. They don't drink our water except maybe on a vacation. I wonder: did the state in a systematic study of all towns finally get to "W" and discover in their bureaucratic compassion that here is a whole aggrieved population with needs long neglected? Or, did some state official on a summer visit to our town have a bad water day that got us the benefit of his attention? If the state is in fact acting as a conduit and mouthpiece for suffering citizens, they should make that clear, publish the pile of complaints they have received.

Not long ago an analogous situation came up with regard to seafood. The state produced new seafood regulations which, without anything changing on the local scene, where we have been harvesting seafood for centuries, instantaneously determined Wellfleet seafood processing to be a problem. This was not, from what I can tell, a case of the regulations coming in response to an epidemic of people—or even one person—getting sick from Wellfleet seafood, which in fact has a longstanding record of excellence. No, somebody whose job it is to come up with regulations came up with these and produced the problem.

Am I saying nobody in Wellfleet has experienced any water difficulties? No. Some with marginally high nitrate readings have for years been employing the easy, cheap, commonsense solution of getting readily available bottled water (following millions in the city who just don't trust urban water). Given the availability of this solution they have not experienced the water as a problem.

The local experience of a local problem might prompt all kinds of solutions besides that massive overhaul of the whole system the state is thrusting on us. Eight million bucks, even interest-free, is a lot of money for a town of this size. But beyond the money, public hearings in the past have made it clear it is the prevailing sense of the situation here that the current system, while not ideal, is a sort of reality check on the true limits to growth here and that a public water system will almost certainly encourage unwanted development, a much larger problem than the occasional high nitrate reading. (We could start chlorinating our ponds to handle the burgeoning summer crowds, but I doubt that would be a popular suggestion either.)

When it comes to water, there are lots of places worse off than this sandbar with its limited aquifer. Tiny islands in the Caribbean too flat to wring rain from clouds get along with catchment systems—rooftops with downspouts leading to cisterns, whole hillsides paved to collect runoff. If individuals don't want to go the bottled water route, they might want to look at such alternative systems, getting it from the sky rather than the ground, since we get much steadier rainfall than most of the Caribbean.

In any case, locals actually suffering a problem are in a better position for coming up with a creative and appropriate solution than those who would impose one from outside.

What we have here is dueling proverbs: shall we let the town's sleeping dog lie? Or accept the state's gift horse? This is one gift horse (if an 8 million dollar debt, even if interest free, can really be called a gift) this town will be carefully scrutinizing at town meeting on Jan. 31, lest it turn out to be a Trojan horse.

NEW COW ON THE FARM

SEEMS LIKE THERE'S ALWAYS one kind of wild thing or another making the headlines around here (surrounded as we are by the wilderness of the sea). If not a tangled Right Whale, then cold-stunned Kemp-Ridley turtles or disoriented dolphins getting themselves stranded. Usually the story is: Kindly humans lend helping hand to fellow species in trouble.

Now it's horseshoe crabs making the front page. But this time, instead of a bumbling wild thing getting hugged, snuggled in blankets, escorted gently back out to sea, the story is that the crabs would be doing just fine except for human intervention. We grind them up for bait. We drain them of their blood to produce a medically useful derivative. (In this latter, more defensible use, they are returned, after being relieved of most of their precious bodily fluids, to the bosom of their families; the procedure kills only about 10 percent of them—an acceptable rate of loss, we are told.)

With the prominent local coverage, we have been alerted that, what with one use or another, horseshoe crabs are disappearing at an alarming rate. From 1984 to 1999 at a local site, the population declined more than 80 percent. After 350 million years of survival success, one of the most successful models ever to come off the evolutionary assembly line is suddenly threatened. Whatever killed off the dinosaurs—asteroid, global cooling, failure to invent coffee—didn't faze the crabs, but now that we have finally come up with a way to make a buck out of them, they are suddenly in big trouble.

If, as sometimes seems true, our love for other species only kicks in when we have wiped out most of them, the horseshoe crab's time to get some of that good TLC has arrived. People are calling the decimation of this species a tragedy. Environmental groups are coming to its defense, the Audubon Society asking for a moratorium on harvesting them.

Why do we care? Why not just exploit them to extinction and move on to the next species? Well, for one thing, although their life may not look all that great to the casual observer—cold, wet, gritty, a diet consisting of sea worms—the species savvy that has enabled them to last so long ought to get them a little respect from an upstart species such as ourselves with our unerring instinct for self-destruction. But the selfish reason is that they are an interesting part of life around here. For decades I have seen them moseying about in the shallows in Wellfleet harbor where I keep my sailboat. What I like about them is that they have always been such a low profile, beneath-the-radar sort of creature. They had, as far as I knew, just not gotten caught up in our system, either as a consumer (they apparently just do not hanker for premium ice creams, designer sneakers, $500 snowboards) or a consumable (they are all shell and no meat). The essence of their high species IQ was that they had contrived somehow to be non-exploitable.

Why do we care about these lowly VW bugs (the original ones) of the creature world? They are not featured as singers on best selling albums like whales, there are no Crab Watch boats, they are not cuddly or dazzling conversationalists like dolphins. What's to love?

Only their otherness, their exotic nature itself. The fact that, until recently, anyway, they were not headline material. There are fewer and fewer places on the Earth that are genuinely away from it all, away from us. The most remote tribes are wearing T-shirts with logos, have been eco-toured and made the subject of documentaries and otherwise appropriated by the dominant culture. But right here in our own harbor, right underfoot, we have this bizarre, ancient race of beings, like living time machines, a conduit to the dinosaurs and beyond.

Why care? It is just refreshing to have creatures that are beyond us—a world beyond our sway.

And so I am sorry to see the horseshoe crabs on the front page. It doesn't bode well. And it changes their meaning. However the empowered agencies end up managing the exploitation of the crabs—perhaps eliminating or limiting the use as bait but permitting the medical use—a major result will be that we will have learned to see yet another fellow species as a resource. When all the crabs in our harbor have been banded (so they can be given time to build up a new blood supply) it will be a different seaside, a different world. It will mean the horseshoe crab, which has for so long avoided being useful to us, has joined the cow, the chicken, the horse, the dog— the fish in the sea, in this era of regulated fishing;   even   the   wolves   re-introduced   into Yellowstone—as just another managed species.

Who will be the one to say we should put the interests of crabs over those of our own species? And yet it is sad to see them becoming, in effect, the latest cow on the farm.

CAN'T HAPPEN HERE

SELF-CONGRATULATION was the order of the evening at a recent meeting sponsored by the Wellfleet Forum. The meeting, attended by a considerably higher percentage of African Americans than are usually seen at such affairs on the Outer Cape, grew out of community concern following the February incident in which Wellfleet police pulled a gun on Mamadou Sow, a visiting African student staying with a family in Wellfleet. No doubt also on the minds of those present was a possible case of racial profiling on the part of Eastham police several weeks a few weeks later. There was a panel consisting of Wellfleet's police chief and Sow's Wellfleet host.

Speaker after speaker started out by saying how hopeful it was that we had come together like this, white and black, to start the healing. But when it came to actual discussion of the event that was the cause of our coming together—the possibility, shocking to some, that in our village with the liberal reputation the police could act in a racist fashion—there was virtually no movement toward understanding.

All the African-American speakers and most of the others made it clear that they believe police use racial profiling—assuming suspicion because of race—on a regular basis and that the Wellfleet incident is no exception. One man told of being stopped by police in his BMW and greeted with the words, "Where did you get this car?" This instance of racial profiling allegedly occurred in Provincetown but I don't think the speaker was trying to draw a distinction between the two Outer Cape towns.

On the other hand, the police officer who first encountered Sow got up and, apparently in all sincerity, said (in essence): The papers have been misleading; believe me, race had nothing to do with this. His chief, while completely agreeing that racial profiling happens all the time in general, was quite clear: Not in this case, not in his department. While he can't control what his officers are thinking and feeling, he said, he can and does instruct them to disregard race when it comes to their activities as public servants. End of story.

Fairly early on, the moderator stated that it had been decided, or hoped, that the discussion would not focus on the actual incident, no doubt to avoid hard feelings which might set back the desired healing of the community over this upsetting event and there was a general reluctance to "point the finger." But the question is: Can there be healing when there is still absolute disagreement as to what occurred? Most people who heard the facts as given in the newspapers believe the police's behavior did involve some element of racism; the officers involved say it did not. The meeting did nothing to change or explore this standoff.

Did those attending the meeting agree, for the sake of healing, to disagree? I didn't get that impression.

No doubt we would all agree that there is such a thing as a justifiable, nonracist suspicion of a minority person as well as a racist suspicion. But we need to understand the difference. If, as the officer said, this was nonracist, then those many people to whom it appeared racist from newspaper accounts need to have that view corrected and to understand just how what appeared to be racist was not racist. If, on the other hand, there was a racist component, then we—the police especially—need to know in precisely what nuances of perception and judgment and action it was racist.

Well into the evening, Sow rose to speak with a perspective perhaps available only to one not of this continent. He spoke of our burgeoning prison population, the disproportionate percent of African Americans in that population, the scandal of what has been declared statistical proof of racism within our law enforcement system. Given these facts and the picture of systematic racism they paint, Sow seemed to be saying that the burden of proof lies heavily with the police.

Maybe we can't ever recover anything as grand as The Truth of the February incident, but it seems important to be able to do a little better in the next update of this town's history than: "Something happened on the Wellfleet bike path in 2000. A lot of people thought it was racist, and the police say it wasn't."

Unless we put more effort into it than we did at the meeting, community healing is likely to remain a pretty sentiment. The Wellfleet police chief's assertion that what he knows to be true of police procedure in general is not true in his department cannot be allowed to stand as the last word on this subject. Neither can the feel-good reiteration of fine ideals and heartfelt hopes.

HONEYMOON OVER

DON'T GET ME WRONG: I love wildlife as much as the next person. It wasn't I who wrote that letter to a local paper advocating kicking the plovers off the beach in favor of volleyball. I swerve, within reason, for deer and squirrels—and a bit beyond reason for chipmunks, which have always seemed a whole nuther world of cute from their loutish cousins.

It is true that I don't go as far as my sister, who blesses her fellow being the mosquito even as it sucks her life's blood. But you would have to say that like a lot of Outer Capers, I am very much into the Romance of the Wild— at least of the wild and cute.

Recently there has been a big uproar over the shooting of ten coyotes to protect terns and plovers. The U.S. Fish and Wildlife Service, playing god, decided some coyotes had to die to protect the more endangered species. There have been protests and angry letters. Up to now I, too, have fancied the idea of coyotes making the local scene. I had coyotes in more or less the same category as the dolphins, horseshoe crabs and Kemp-Ridley turtles, endangered wild things that made my heart sing. An underdoggie making a comeback.

I say I have liked the idea of a coyote comeback because I haven't actually seen one yet; they are still more of a rumor for me than anything else. But neighbors have seen them; one saw what looked like a pack of them. There are reports of cats disappearing under suspicious circumstances, a story that coyotes have wiped out the feral cats of Provincetown. Now that it appears there may be a real threat to our own cat, of whom I am rather fond, I find myself in conflict. The image of a coyote chowing down on Lily is decidedly disturbing. Suddenly, it seems, coyotes are no longer the underdog; they are turning our cat into an underdog.

I think what's happening for a lot of us is that, with the increase in coyote population, this particular wild thing is being bumped from the category of the Romance of the Wild into the category of us vs. them realism. The love affair with wildlife is being challenged by the realities of sharing territory. Back in an earlier stage of development of this continent when we were threatened daily by the wild we had little time or inclination for romancing it. Since wild animals ceased to be a threat, usually because we reduced their numbers to a fraction of the original, we have found our lives enhanced by entertaining the poetry of the wild.

A lot of us like the idea of the wild and cheer on the wild creatures that are always making the news out here. But our wilderness is the sea around us and whales and dolphins and sea turtles and piping plovers don't threaten our house pets.

And if we have reason to worry about our slower cats and smaller dogs, it must be crossing the minds of some parents that their toddlers would be a lot easier target for a coyote than a cat, and would—just guessing here— make a juicier meal. I have read comments by purported experts on coyote history to the effect that coyotes have rarely messed with humankind. Still, if I had a toddler, I would be thinking about putting a corral around him.

For most of us, this is new moral terrain. We don't feel comfortable taking an anti-wild position. Probably the wilderness advocates of Earth First! would say: Let the coyotes eat the pets—look what domestic cats do to rodent and bird populations. Some of the more committed Deep Ecologists probably wouldn't mind if coyotes thinned the human population just a bit, either. But most of us are attached to our house pets and toddlers.

What's a cat owner to do? Move the cat indoors full-time, as coyote advocates suggest? But that would eliminate the free life in nature that is a certain part of the appeal of a cat. Fence out the coyotes? "The heck with these defensive measures," says my wife, who is from upstate New York and more in touch with her pioneer roots than some of us. "We should call Town Hall, get them to offer a bounty." She begins to inventory the considerable, underused arsenal our son has been assembling over the years—BB gun, crossbow, blowgun, etc.—wondering just what it would take to protect our cat from the coyote menace. (Hell, we'll paintball the critters into submission.) Seems a little extreme to me, a downstate guy, at this point, but with such thoughts thinkable even in jest, the honeymoon with the coyote would seem to be over.

LAME DUCKS

THE *CAPE COD TIMES'* massive series last month on the Cape's historic housing crisis was appropriately depressing. The gist: because of the second home market almost all Cape housing is now beyond the reach of almost all of the sort of people who have traditionally chosen to live here, the mix of working middle-class, lumpen proletariat artists, former beatniks and hippies that has always characterized the Cape community. As a result, although the Cape may look more or less like its old self, its soul is or soon will be completely different.

It was a soberingly dose of realism. But after the initial swoon into the slough of despond, the question came up for me: If things are so bad, why doesn't life here in Wellfleet feel so bad? And I realized (realizing the obvious is one of my strong points) that one of the things left out of the series was the very important fact that a lot of us who are here to read that series, although we share the socio-economic situation of those threatened with homelessness or leaving the Cape, form a community of those who bought their piece of paradise back when it was affordable. That's why we are here shaking our heads about the *Times* series and others less fortunate aren't.

It is sobering to think that if my wife and I hadn't in 1982, in a lazy, tentative way decided on one of our typical visits to Wellfleet (camping at the Audubon, commuting to the ponds) to see what was available in the way of building lots, on the off-chance we might be able to scrape together a downpayment on one, we would have missed the boat. Had this impulse happened to strike us even a year later I wouldn't be here now writing this column.

And if you are thinking: Hey, give yourself credit for making a timely investment move, you are giving us more credit than we deserve. This was a purely a purchase of love, an expression of our ancient romance with this place. We found an oversize lot in the woods for 19 thou, said to each other, Wow, that's not a half bad price for a nice bit of our place. Borrowing the $6,000 downpayment from my sister and putting the rest plus our owner-built cottage on a home equity loan, we managed it. Had we had even a suspicion of the mid-'80s real estate boom about to descend, we would probably have found a way to swing another lot or two. Never crossed our minds. We were still framing our cottage only a few months after buying the lot when prices started going crazy and within a year or so our lot, judged by comparable properties, was worth five or six times what we had paid for it.

Had we come to town looking for land even a few months after we did—or any time since—we would have just kept on driving; we would have been out of luck.

So we feel lucky to be here. We look around at friends most of whom bought in the nick of time, not knowing at the time it was the nick. On the one hand we constitute a sort of "intentional" community of people who didn't come here because of a job that happened to be in the neighborhood or because it was a good investment, but rather out of affection for this place. On the other hand we are for the most part a completely accidental community, beneficiaries of the sheer accident of timing.

And of course it changes the essential nature of this place to realize that we are economic anachronisms. This was an affordable, funky place when we bought—that's why we bought, that's how we bought. Now economically it should be grouped with Westport, Brookline, Carmel, Aspen, places with a whole other cultural meaning.

There are repercussions for our children, who, will in all probability be unable to buy into the town they grew up loving; even if they can it will not for a moment be the town they knew.

The people at the library or coffee place during the offseason are the same familiar faces, our community still functions in much the old way; the woods and ponds and ocean all seem unchanged. But emerging from your own house after reading the *Times* series you gaze out on an alien economic landscape. It's more than trophy houses or new developments with too many houses standing empty most of the year—it's a new reality that changes the meaning of everything.

ELECTRONIC CITIZENSHIP

SOME OF MY BEST FRIENDS are non-resident taxpayers. Honest.

A sort of non-resident taxpayers' revolt in Wellfleet is in the making. On Aug. 30 there will be an organizational meeting of those wishing to play more of a role in town affairs. Some of this sizeable group of people who own houses here but who live most of their lives elsewhere— more than half of all our taxpayers, according to the newspaper article I read—want to have an advisory voice, as part-timers, which seems a laudable and useful thing.

But at least some want more. They contemplate petitioning for the same right to vote at regular town meetings enjoyed by fulltime residents. One of the leaders of the local movement, making a presentation at a recent meeting of the board of selectmen, said that e-mail now even makes feasible regular participation on committees and town boards.

Thus doth the specter of electronic citizenship raise its head.

Fundamental to the traditional notion of a residency requirement for voting is the concept of citizenship as an embodied activity, a recognition that there is something essential to the democratic process about simply spending most of your time in a place. There 's the old saying: you can't be in more than one place at a time. And that being the case, it has always been important where you decided to be most of the time, where you committed to living your life.

It used to be, until a few years ago, that a decision to move to a small town like this one meant moving, lock, stock and barrel (and color TV and VCR) from the old place. You could not be in two places at once. You left your old situation, and threw in your lot with other self-marginalizing folks who had traded in their chances for a real career and big money (yeah, right) for scenery and smalltown community.

Now computers would persuade us otherwise, that we can be in as many places as we have time to click on icons. That you can, in essence, be citizens of two or more different places at once. Ubiquity seems within our grasp.

With telecommuting, you can decide to move your body here while still, in some important sense, more or less staying there. Now we confront the proposal of electronic citizenship.

But there is no substitute for the old-fashioned idea of residency, physical presence in a place over a period of time—getting rained on with everyone else by our kind of rain, dealing along with other full-time denizens not only with the summer crowds but the winter sparseness of population, fully subjected to the tradeoff between a more limited job market and the sense of freedom of a small, rural, edge place.

I was surprised to learn from one who often knows this sort of thing that residency is not at present required by state law for membership on committees. But showing up for meetings is required, which I suppose for all practical purposes has amounted to a residency requirement.

Being present in the form of an emailed opinion seems a very different thing. Making public statements and casting votes while facing those whose lives will be affected by the decision you make, whom you will be seeing at the coffee place, at the post office, is difficult, but has always seemed an essential part of the democratic process. Voting or commenting by email (even accompanied by a picture of yourself sitting elsewhere, as may in the not too distant future become possible) is too easy, lacking in fundamental constraints, elements of traditional participation.

The traditional logic of the residency requirement comes down to shared condition. You could argue, I suppose, that all human beings—and other creatures as well—have a stake in what goes on in Wellfleet (it being "one world" and we all being brothers and sisters, as we are informed by the cliches) and should all vote in our town meeting—that we should all vote in all town meetings everywhere. Perhaps, so such an argument might continue, the actual fulltime dwellers in a town are too close to the trees to see the forest, too immersed in our own situation, too interested, in the sense of biased, to vote well. Maybe, in fact, we should actually go out and recruit our votership, as we do increasingly our town officials, from elsewhere, people who could see our situation with the proper dispassion and disinterest.

But here's a vote for the traditional idea that only those with a fulltime stake in as well as fulltime knowledge of the situation should be qualified to vote. Where we choose to park our bods still counts, or should, even in a world increasingly diluted by electronics.

TRANSCENDING OUR GROCERY SHOPPING DICHOTOMY

WHY SHOULD A WELLFLEET resident get his knickers in a twist at the thought of a Stop & Shop moving into a town 10 miles up the highway? There would even be certain advantages to a Wellfleetian: a Stop & Shop in North Truro would cut a few minutes off the weekly trek for serious grocery shopping to the big box in Orleans.

Another point in its favor: like that asteroid with our planet's number on it, if it hits Truro it is less likely to hit us. I ought to rejoice. But I don't. And apparently, to judge by the letters section of local papers, I'm not alone. For something that is still in the brainstorming stage, and for which no official applications have been made to town boards, the idea of making our down-Cape neighbor a mecca for grocery shoppers has caused a lot of spirited debate.

The arguments pro and con are quickly summarized: convenience, price and selection vs. traffic congestion and erosion of that intangible, town character. And of course both sides are right: the big box supermarket would be convenient—as for that matter would a Home Depot or Chilis—and yes, it would wreak havoc with the traditional, rural character of the town and the Outer Cape in general.

Once again with the Stop & Shop proposal we seem stuck in the old dichotomy: no new business at all vs. inappropriate business. This tiresome standoff needs transcending.

Here in Wellfleet for a long time we have been served by a small, colorful grocery, which, although far better than nothing and certainly an important part of the fabric of Main Street, does not even pretend to be a full service, competitive store. I doubt the owner ever complains about his customers doing their serious shopping at the megastore in Orleans. It only makes economic sense. It's just the way things are now, the big guys can offer price and selection; that brightly lit hangar-like space is just the way a serious grocery looks these days.

It's as if we simply can't imagine anything between the two alternatives, the cute-but-token local store and globalization in the form of the big box store. But there are alternatives to the ubiquitous, lookalike franchises that dominate American life.

Take the world of coffee. Starbucks is almost synonymous with the upscale coffee scene in this country and it does produce a good cup of coffee. But right here in Wellfleet we have the Outer Cup, a local coffee using locally roasted beans to produce a good, rich brew in a setting in which locals feel comfortable hanging out. A good cross section of locals have beaten a path to its door (even though that door has had trouble settling down to one location). When it comes to the coffeehouse position in this town, Starbucks need not apply.

Same with our local year-round restaurants. Anyone who regularly patronizes these community mainstays, with their reasonably priced, generously sized lunch specials, and a waitressing style you just don't get in a nationwide franchise, knows McDonalds or Chilis would not be a reasonable substitute.

Seems to me what we need is a grocery version of the local coffee spots and restaurants, something creatively designed to split the difference between the token store and the giant, character-less nonlocal store two towns away. I'm not a professional grocer and I wouldn't presume to tell one how to run his business. But I am an experienced grocery consumer, and here's some of what might keep me shopping at home. Reasonably competitive prices (but they wouldn't have to be as low as a Stop & Shop because of the savings on gas, time, and hassle). Local seafood, fish and produce (maybe more locals could be persuaded to actually grow some). Lively, local help. Creative use of an existing building, if possible (remove all the aisle space taken up in a bigbox store with furniture, drugs, books, hardware, flowers, all of which can be found in specialty shops elsewhere in town, and would you really need the big box?) Keep the scale human; lose those deadening overhead lights. Little touches: a community bulletin board, maybe a small, informal cafe.

One native of my acquaintance says that when she was growing up in Wellfleet in the 40s or '50s there were five, count 'em, five grocery stores in town. For a population at that time of not much over 1000, one third of our present population.

If we could just get beyond the idea that a real, serious grocery store must look like a hangar-like replica of every other megagrocery in the country and created instead a competitive local store with a little charm and a special sense of local needs, I do believe we could learn to live without that weekly commute for groceries.

WE HATE
WHEN WE DO THAT

THIS IS THE KIND OF PLACE where place, and threats to place, are a big story. I mean a *big* story. Usually, newspaper stories are measured in column inches. The *Cape Cod Times'* recent three-part series on Truro's growth spurt invites measurement in square feet (about 10, I calculate). This is more than a wakeup call. This is a billboard. Truro—and other towns on the Outer Cape in roughly the same situation—would have to say we have been given fair warning.

A Truro plumber and builder are quoted early on in the series as saying they may have made a mistake when they worked to defeat a building cap proposal at town meeting two years ago. "On the one hand," says the builder, "[the growth] feeds my family and, on the other, it makes it so I don't really have much interest in being around here much longer. It's just too much." Having defeated the cap, the builders have so much work that it's driving them nuts. And as they drive around town they can't help but be disgusted at what they see.

It is refreshing to hear this honesty: You make your bed, you have to lie in it—or move to Maine, where you get to make it again, maybe do a better job. But others quoted in the story don't want to take this sort of responsibility. "Truro, I believe, is just destined to become the Carmel of the East coast," says the town's building commissioner.

What's destiny got to do with it? Sure, the handwriting's on the wall, but if you look closely, it's our handwriting. Neither destiny, nor El Nino, nor the international commie conspiracy is pushing the Outer Cape in the direction of Aspen or Carmel or other towns-as-cautionary tales. It's us, the voting citizens of these towns.

The plumber and builder admit to being part of the problem. Another part is the 6,000-square foot house, widely criticized, according to the article, as a trophy house (by definition, a house too big and show offy by community standards). Destiny is not building this trophy house. The neighbors and others walking the beach know exactly who is responsible for transforming the Truro dunescape and they have not been shy about letting the perpetrators know their feelings about it. According to one trophy house owner, "It's too big, they say. We've actually had people come up off the beach and confront the builders—sort of insulting them and saying, 'how dare you.'"

Diana Worthington, a lifelong resident, said she is appalled by the number of trophy house in Truro. "They're so out of place," she said. "They look so ghastly. It's a disgusting scene. You wonder what's happening to our town."

Even the owner of a trophy house admits: "I've noticed such a change in the last 10 years."

One of Billy Crystal's famous "Saturday Night Live" skits was the "I-hate-when-I-do-that" routine. He would in some detail tell his working buddy about how, for no apparent reason, he stuck his finger in the toaster or whacked his knee with a hammer, ending with the line, "I hate when I do that." The buddy would nod in agreement, "Yeah, that would hurt." The Truro citizens discussed in the article seem to be in much the same situation as the Crystal sado-masochist.

Trophy house owner: "Gee, I built this huge house totally out of character for the area, it ruins the traditional view of the dunes and has my neighbors insulting my builders. I hate when I do that."

Tradesmen fight anti-growth zoning and notice all the ugly growth around town: "I hate when I do that."

Town officials, guided by fatalistic thinking, fail to take initiative in crafting creative zoning safeguards and then point to unwanted development as evidence that inexorable forces are pushing us toward the sort of future no one really wants. "We hate when we do that."

Of course, builders and developers could limit the take and reap the reward of a town they actually enjoy living in. Planning boards and other town officials could start seeing themselves as the agents of destiny instead of its victims and start doing the necessary planning. Those about to build oversized houses in prominent places could save themselves and others a lot of pain by thinking twice about the effects of their actions.

Or we can go on taking the towns we love for their livability, spaciousness and modesty of scale and, by omission and commission, turning them into something else again. But we hate when we do that.

OUR OPM PROBLEM

ACCORDING TO FRIENDS strategically placed in the world of high finance the big thing for 20-somethings these days is no longer keg parties and wet T-shirt contests but rather getting on the millionaire track. (Actually my source for this as for all other matters is "Doonesbury," where I get as much info about the outside world as I can stand.) The deal is you come up with a business plan, you get OPM (Other People's Money) to invest in your idea, then after about a month you do an IPO (initial public offering of stock), where you make your bundle and then retire when the investors find out you never really intended to produce anything.

All of which sounds wonderful, but it seems to work better in Silicon Valley than here on the Outer Cape. It's not that we have trouble attracting investors—we have a good product here in this charming little town. No, our problem is that we have more OPM than we can use. The OPM thing isn't working for us.

At a recent meeting of the Wellfleet Town Forum it became clear that our big problem is not lack of open space, not water quality, not even our inability to get beyond a one night stand stage with a town administrator. No, our big problem is OPM. Too many people from where money is made showing their appreciation for our product by lavishing it on us and driving up prices.

The assumption has always been that if we keep our town open and rural, say with a land bank, that our quality of life (QOL) will be safe. But the theme at the Forum was the threat to the other key component of life here: our liveability. This used to be not only a pretty place but an easy going, affordable one for artists, writers, hippies, dropouts, working families and other varieties of the unrich. It is quickly becoming too expensive.

People spoke of their grown kids not being able to return to their hometown to settle here. Others pointed out that while this has always been a great place to bring up children, the elementary school population is down about a third since a few years ago. It is shrinking because families can't afford to live here. We are becoming a place transformed by OPM, other people's money coming here, building trophy homes, second homes, changing the demographics of town.

So, if the Land Bank is the way we fight overdevelopment, how do we keep OPM from ruining our QOL, pushing us the way of Nantucket or Aspen? I suppose we could erect signs at our borders on Route 6—WELL-HEELED: YOUR MONEY NOT GOOD HERE. But no, we've got to be cleverer than that. Like a woman deliberately dressing in baggy, dowdy clothes to discourage unwanted male interest, we have to find ways of making ourselves less desirable.

For instance, a short time ago we passed a new zoning law setting up a light commercial ghetto to get unsightly work apparatus out of neighborhoods. Wrong approach. Repeal the commercial zone, get the neighborhoods back to looking like places OPM will be less interested in investing.

Our token efforts at affordable housing have similarly involved ghetto thinking: locate a few units off by themselves somewhere where they won't contaminate other neighborhoods. Bad idea. Rather: spread affordable housing throughout town. Discourage the wealthy from thinking they can get away from the less wealthy (the old mansion on the hill model). Be the homogeneous community we have always been.

Instead of passing bylaws to sanitize our neighborhoods, get back to the comfortable, liveable look of a working and none-too-well off population. Old cars kept for spare parts rusting in sideyards; piles of shellfish byproducts and other possibly useful stuff; chicken coops, sheds, working vegetable gardens.

We can use zoning to make a place in which only the wealthy can feel comfortable. Or we can use it to be the kind of town those looking for a trophy house site will just drive through on their way to a more secure-looking investment.

A living, breathing, fully functional downtown such as ours was not many decades ago has a way of turning into just the sort of cute, picture postcard downtown that attracts OPM. Maybe, if we get desperate enough, we should invite McDonalds, golden arches and all, to contaminate pristine Main Street. That would take the edge off our picture postcard desirability.

CALL OF THE WILD

HOW ARE WE TO THINK about the fire started in the National Seashore in Wellfleet by partying teens during the summer?

Coming up with just the right tone in dealing with the young perps ought to be a tough one for this town because of our wild and free self-image. Traditionally many Wellfleetians stay here, return here or wash ashore here believing this town to be less regulated, less uptight than the urbs and suburbs of mainland America. Paradoxically, the federal taking and regulation of over 60% of our town for a park has preserved all this wide open space in which to be wild and free. (If development had been allowed to proceed at a normal pace over the past 40 years it is doubtful there would now be left any woods to set on fire.)

Having a party in a wild spot in the middle of the woods might not in fact seem a crime to a lot of the grownups around here, including some of the parents of the kids involved. Such a celebration might, in fact, seem exactly what you should want to do with all that part of our town kept wild. What, some might say, is all that wild territory good for if not occasionally to be wild in it, howl at the moon, beat on pots and pans...and, yes, even build a fire. Sure we can lawfully walk and drive the sand roads, swim in secluded ponds but what about all the woods off the beaten track? Doesn't it call out? Why should we be the only creature hereabouts not to use it?

More than one of my fellow adult citizens, when I have brought up the subject has said, Well, as a matter of fact...they have on occasion seized the impulse, grabbed a sleeping bag, and spent the night out there where the wild things are.

I also know of numerous unauthorized rituals over the years conducted in the dark of night at various pond and dune and woods sites—locals answering the call of the wild.

I have one friend who seems constitutionally unable to swim with a bathing suit on. She believes of our local ponds what Gary Snyder the poet wrote of a special river in the Sierra Nevada foothills: it would be a sacrilege to immerse in these waters with a suit on. I have no doubt she would put her love of her favorite pond up against that of the uniformed ones who come to test its water...and hassle naked swimmers. It is, she probably would say, her love of the pond, mixed with her love of feeling her body in it, that makes her again and again break the rule against joining fellow critters in celebrating the wild in the altogether.

And of course it would never occur to these grownup perpetrators that the occasional bending or breaking of a NS rule means they don't respect the wilderness. On the contrary.

I have been told by those close to the situation that like many Wellfleet kids, those responsible for the accidental fire regard themselves as especially careful and respectful of the environment. After all, they say, we are 'Fleetians. We have grown up in this town. We love its wildness. I am told that in fact the fire was built carefully, trenched around, with good campfire technique, and kept modest in size. And when it nevertheless went awry, not doused thoroughly enough given the very dry conditions

—when, yes, a mistake was made—these kids were as mortified as anybody. And not just because of the hot water they were in. But because they had hurt one of the things they love most about their town.

None of which is to say that the fire wasn't a serious problem. At the very least it—and the fire road crashed through to put it out—messes up those woods for others. It could conceivably have threatened property and even lives. But it makes a difference to me that it didn't, apparently, result from childish stupidity or destructiveness or arrogance but rather from the sort of impulse a lot of us feel and sometimes act on, really not a bad impulse but, in a sense that we understand around here, a good one. (Unlike dogs pooping on the beach or using personal watercraft, building a fire in our outback, at least in its unaccidental form doesn't pollute others' enjoyment of the outdoors. The whole point is to get away from other people.)

As for our attitude toward and treatment of the young people who were not careful enough in this case, I hope we will resist the temptation to take the comfortable, simplistic way out and file it under right and wrong, good and bad, law-and-order adults vs. lawless kids. In a town like this with the oxymoron of regulated wilderness at its very center, it is more complicated than that.

And maybe, because it is silly to have laws that really don't reflect the beliefs of a lot of the people most affected, fires should not be prohibited, in the off-season anyway, at least for locals in a town where wildness is a local value and where we all have a stake in being careful.

OUTSIDER FETISH; OR, BETTER THE T.A. YOU DON'T KNOW

IN THE LATEST DEVELOPMENT of Wellfleet's ever-so-interesting town politics, there is a movement afoot to rehire the Town Administrator we just, in effect, fired only a couple of months ago.

The selectmen who seemed most displeased with the performance of Bill Dugan are history, swept out by expressively large margins in recent elections, the new board seems to have different ideas about lots of things, so why not the question of T.A.? Mr. Dugan needs the job, would like to stay in a town he has apparently gotten attached to, and there is a petition circulating with a growing number of signatures of people who apparently have gotten attached to him. There is the feeling that to rehire, essentially to keep, Dugan would be a healing thing in a town that has been seen in recent years as a revolving door for its top administrator.

The reconsideration of Bill Dugan is less about this particular person than the themes of fetish and scapegoat, flip sides of the same unfortunate phenomenon. There has been a tendency in the last decade or two, even in a town which has traditionally cherished the values of localness and independence, to see outsideness, non-localness, as being a requirement for key hirings such as building inspector and Town Administrator. It's as if there is some magic associated with not being from here that is a prerequisite to such positions. The corollary: insideness pollutes, acts an anti-credential.

Bill Dugan himself, chosen over numerous other outsider candidates in a meticulous process, was just such a magical stranger not long ago, riding in on his white horse after having, for all we knew, slain all the dragons in the small town in Vermont where he had most recently administered. But now he is tainted by having been in our midst for a while. He knows us a bit, we know him. He is no longer the outsider he was.

Meanwhile, the strangers line up to apply for his job, every one of whose resumes include that intriguing credential of not knowing anything about this place. This making a fetish of the outsider has everything to do with the pre-dominate ideology of professionalism. The professional is the hired gun, the outsider par excellence. Fly him in to consult for a day or two, ship him out again. Any more immersion in local situation and he will get his powder wet and be no good to anybody.

The other side of the professional fetish is the ever-handy scapegoat—fetish in reverse. If things aren't going right, get rid of him. Simply by being here, getting intimate with the local scene, the outsider loses the essential ingredient of professional detachment, no matter how qualified he seemed just a short time ago. Familiarity seems indeed to breed contempt, even in a town in which familiarity is usually a valued quality.

As the petition to reconsider the present T.A. suggests, familiarity has more advantages than disadvantages. It will take any new outside hiree months to get up to speed on local issues, and by that time he or she will no doubt have lost the allure of professional aloofness. We will once again have to make do with a human relationship with all the limits and disappointments thereof.

LEGISLATED DIVERSITY IN THE LATTER DAYS OF THE FORMER BEER CAPITAL OF THE WESTERN WORLD

THE *TIMES'* RECENT SERIES on the Cape's housing crisis, which featured Aspen, Colorado's approach to its housing crisis, got me thinking about my old connection to that famous mountain resort.

Around 30 years ago, some friends and I hit Aspen on a classic, Kerouac-inspired, cross-country road trip after a summer on the West Coast. A major goal was to score a case of Coors. According to our information, Coors was not at that time available east of the Rockies. Aspen was rumored to be the prime source. We stout-spirited, brew-minded crossers of deserts had convinced ourselves that Coors had some beer magic that put it in another world from the likes of Ballantine, Budweiser, Miller and other standbys of that benighted era. We came, we saw the refreshing slopes of Aspen's mountains, the charming mining-town Victorian storefronts; we scored the case. With great discipline, we left it unopened the whole 2,000 miles back to the East Coast. It was doled out can by can over the next several months, as I remember, on occasions of great moment and ceremony. We were ourselves treated with a certain amount of gravity and respect, as befits those who have been to a Sacred Source.

I wasn't, in those days, much into pondering the fate of small resorts, but if I had, my thinking would have gone: Any place with all that old mining-town charm, surrounded by all those great skiing mountains, that is also the Coors capital of the universe, has a lot to recommend it. That was in fact my line on Aspen for a few years.

Things began to change. For one thing, pretty soon you could buy Coors anywhere and, despite the attempts of TV ads to keep it associated with the Rockies, the magical Coors/Aspen connection was lost. Meanwhile, through the '70s and '80s, Aspen's stock as a place of genuine character nose-dived as stories appeared about this or that Hollywood celeb buying a second home there, making the erstwhile funky mountain town seem more and more like another Hollywood set.

For years, in writing about the character of Cape Cod, I have used Aspen as a convenient, well-known cautionary tale of a town that had lost its soul to second-home gentrification. So I was surprised to see Aspen being cited in the *Times'* series as an example of forward-looking, positive action. Turns out that things got so bad back in the '90s, with the Californicating of Aspen pushing virtually all housing beyond the reach of non-millionaires (median house price an obscene $2.7 million), they reached a crisis. Loss of the traditional, liveable town character was one problem; but at a more practical level it became clear that those needed to run a town—town employees, waitresses, carpenters, ski lift operators—could not afford to live anywhere near Aspen.

The solution: progressive legislation taxing house sales for an affordable housing kitty and requiring developers to make an astounding 60 percent of any new development affordable. The result, according to the *Times'* story, is that of Aspen's total housing stock, almost 40 percent is kept affordable—that is, not subject to market forces.

By comparison with Aspen's solutions, Cape Cod's are pathetic; no Cape town has more than a token number of affordable housing units. On the other hand, this is a place where until very recently an unregulated housing market seemed to work OK by itself without such measures. A town like Wellfleet, for instance, just seemed naturally to have enough plumbers, electricians, waitresses and fishermen to serve local needs. It's not something anyone thought about. It just seemed that all little towns just naturally used to contain people willing and able to do what needed to be done to keep the town going and make enough money doing it to be able to afford to live there. It's an important part of what we mean when we use the term "community."

The Aspen solution, the artificial creation of a diverse community, smacks of legislating a worker ghetto: working people tolerated in affordable housing for the sole purpose of serving the multimillionaires. The class vibes must be weird.

The point of the *Times'* series is that, because of the second-home market craziness, we may be reaching the point of needing to legislate diversity and community character ourselves; and Aspen offers a solution. But it is hard to admit that we have reached that point. One wonders what living in such an artificially structured community would feel like.

TRURO GOLF
AND THE TALIBAN

WELL, SUCH IS THE LOT of the columnist. Here I was, all set to write a piece on one of my favorite topics, the importance of indigenousness (such a cumbersome and yet scrunchy word), especially the tradition of Outer Cape small-town self-sufficiency when, wouldn't you know it, my theme got globalized to smithereens. Specifically, I was going to write supporting the effort to keep management of Truro's Highland Links golf course local. But then came the newspaper stories about the Taliban blowing up all the statues in Afghanistan. Clearly, I had either to abandon the localness theme or expand it to include Afghanistan.

But what have the statues of Afghanistan got to do with the golf in Truro, says you. Aha, says I.

The argument for keeping Truro golf in the family came first of all, anecdotally, from my own experience as a golfer—the fact that I am an intensely mediocre golfer doesn't disqualify me from making these observations— that the powers that have been up there have been doing a great job of keeping the course looking good and keeping the prices down. This last, as you non-golfers might not know, makes the course a rare bird in a world in which golf is getting increasingly to be a rich person's sport. I like to think the local golf courses are priced so that the year-round resident of modest means can afford to play here. When the greens fees start exceeding the lift fees in Vermont and you are required, as is becoming common, to pay still more money to rent an electric cart, (which in turn necessitates wearing pale green polyester pants), some golfers are forced to shift to other sports, like bird watching (insert jokes here about birdies and eagles).

Now there is no guarantee that if an outside company were to win the bid to take over management, as a result of throwing the bidding open to all comers as the Seashore threatens to do, it would start nudging Highland in the direction of Pebble Beach, but why take chances? I have a certain amount of faith that locals, just because they are local, might be more likely to keep local pocketbooks and predilections in mind than outsider investors.

Part two of the column was to be a more theoretical defense of localness as a value. Seems to me that the whole notion of *place* depends on localness, on the separation of here from there, of Truro from Wellfleet from Provincetown, of the Outer Cape from elsewhere. Without separateness, you don't have place. Global Village means the end of actual villages like ours. For much of the history of our area that separation has been maintained by inherent limits on transportation and communications. But little by little, technology has chipped away at our essential separateness from the Big World. Phones and radio at first, then TV, then cable TV and dishes which actually produced decipherable pictures. And then, accelerating through the last few years, other agents of electronic ubiquity: the Internet, email, telecommuting, GPS, and cell phones. At some point not long ago we began to feel more on the grid than off. It was One World and damned if we weren't part of it, even if dragged kicking and screaming. Chain stores pressed on us, Dunkin Donuts getting as close as Eastham, Staples in Orleans. Global Village here we come.

And then I saw the story about the locals in Afghanistan determined to dismantle millennia of sculpture— traditional, monumental art that in the view of this outsider seemed part and parcel of that ancient place. And of course what did I want to do? Take management of those sculptures out of local control and give it to an international commission. Damned if I didn't want to globalize the care of those statues.

It didn't take long before I was saying to myself: And I suppose in the name of local control you are happy the management of things in Rwanda was left in local hands? Content that somehow genocide, in a way nonlocals just can't appreciate, worked for them?

And what about local control in Nazi Germany?

You can see how the whole localness theme began to unravel—reality challenging a perfectly lovely theory.

So reluctantly I've got to back off from the defense of local management of golf in Truro based on universally applicable theory. Being one of the locals in this case, I vote for it in this case. On the Outer Cape, more often than not, I'll go with local management. (Oh yeah? And what if the question of the creation of the National Seashore had been left to Charlie Frazier and local sentiment in general?)

OK, OK… How about this: local control is good when my generation of residents are the locals in question. And they make a decision I agree with.

ω ω ω

NOTE: This did not have the irony when it appeared in March it was to take on six months later.

WHAT HAPPENED
IN WELLFLEET?

WHAT JUST HAPPENED in Wellfleet?

A DCPC application process just went rampaging through town. Did anyone get its license plate number?

Remember the Old Pier Road mystery closure episode of a few years back? We woke up one morning to find a fence built in the middle of what had been a turnaround at a traditional access spot used by shellfishermen and others. There was a big uproar, some close questioning of Conscom and the DPW, a hearing, and in short order the fence was taken down and things put more or less back to normal. But I bet if you asked 10 people exactly what happened, what really went down, who got who to do what and why, you would come up with as many stories. The whole thing ended, as things often do in this town, in mystery. Maybe we just don't want to know. Maybe ignorance is, if not bliss, a way of living and letting live, of forgiving and forgetting. Maybe community would suffer if the left hand ever really did find out what the right hand is doing.

When some future Judy Stetson updates the history of this period, how will this DCPC episode be told? At the open session of the selectmen's meeting at which the Planning Board officially announced its decision to withdraw the application to the Cape Cod Commission for a District of Critical Planning Concern designation, a citizen rose to read to the selectmen from the founding document of our country, lest they forget, the lesson they should draw from this DCPC business: That government gets its authority from the consent of the governed. In other words, the withdrawal after several raucous hearings should be viewed as a great victory for democracy and a rebuke to those who dared to try to pull a fast one on we the people.

Certainly the developers, builders, realtors and supporters who were most of the speakers at the DCPC hearings characterized themselves that way: In a few hours we got more than 200 people to sign a petition for withdrawal; no way we are just a special interest group who stands to lose by further regulation. We are the people of this town and we are outraged the Planning Board's doubly undemocratic attempt to involve the Commission in local planning and do it without adequate notice.

But there is another way story could be told. Given almost daily newspaper articles about overdevelopment Capewide, trophy houses, traffic problems, water problems, the Planning Board, like anyone else living here during the past decade, could be excused for believing that in applying for the DCPC it represented the prevailing attitude. Six years ago at Town Meeting we voted in a detailed, thoughtful Local Comprehensive Plan which calls for new zoning to modify the buildout scenario. Like every other town on the Cape, we voted for a Land Bank in order to rescue as many lots as possible from development. By a wide margin in recent Town Meeting votes we have resisted, despite considerable pressure from the state, a public water system which would, it is feared, enable unwanted development downtown. It is not hard to see how the Planning Board might have gotten the idea that most of their fellow citizens believe that something should be done, and done in a hurry, to modify the current growth trajectory.

In other words, it is conceivable that the way the story should be written is: builders, realtors and other self-interested parties packed meetings, heckling and intimidating the P.B. into withdrawing a proposal that was, in fact, in the interest of the majority. It is possible that is the more accurate version of what just happened.

It seems clear the Planning Board made a big mistake in not making an aggressive effort to include more of the town in the decision to apply for the DCPC. Had they done a townwide survey first to demonstrate that this was not just a hunch on its part but that indeed the majority of town does favor DCPC, things might well have gone differently. The building community would not have been able to seize the moral high ground by making a regulation issue into a democracy issue.

If such a survey shows that the majority of town thinks our present zoning regulations, or bylaws the town can come up with without a moratorium, are sufficient regulation, so be it. If, on the other hand, a majority favors a DCPC process, builders, having raised the democracy issue, should themselves submit with grace to the will of the people.

The Old Pier Road controversy concerned only one public water access (although it involved an important principle). But this question of how to go about planning the immediate future of the whole town is too important to leave a mystery. We should find out what we think in an atmosphere other than one of intimidation.

It is important to know what just happened in Wellfleet.

ORIGINAL SIN

I JUST REALIZED this year is the 40th anniversary of the start of the federal intervention in local affairs called the Cape Cod National Seashore.

Not to get all melodramatically biblical about it, but is it not our Original Sin, the failure of this town—of all Outer Cape towns—to support the one conservation measure now widely regarded as most responsible for our present quality of life, our salvation from the overdeveloped fate of much of the rest of the world, including much of the Cape?

Everything I have read suggests that had the issue been left to local self-determination (the Seashore was created by an act of Congress) the two-thirds of our town presently lying fallow would now be developed coast to coast. Does that mean that in this case, if not in the recent case of our DCPC application, the overriding of local control was a good thing? 40 years down the road are we willing to swallow our pride and admit that the best interests of our town were guarded not by the majority of citizens but by a bunch of nonlocal politicians?

If our bitter opposition to the Seashore 40 years ago is our Original Sin, in a neat Hollywood-style, feel-good reversal of the original story, we sinners got kicked *into*

Eden (if Eden can be imagined with seven months of weather during which you definitely want to wear your fur-lined fig leaf).

Of course that happy ending for the undeserving only looks like that with the benefit of hindsight. I wonder just when it was that the territory torn from the town began to look like Eden to the majority. Presumably at those Seashore hearings in the late 50s, 'Fleetians such as Mr. Wellfleet himself, Charlie Frazier, passionately argued another perspective on Eden, one we have a hard time appreciating now: Eden as a sort of prison of rural, underdeveloped innocence from which the only salvation was freedom to develop. The locals in possession of Eden did not welcome a bossy outsider coming along and telling them not to eat that apple; they wanted in fact to be free to eat as many apples as they could gobble, even plant an orchard and make a buck by getting as many others eating them as possible (speaking in biblical symbol-talk here; this wasn't ever great apple territory).

It would be interesting to see what our town would look like now if the Seashore had not locked up most of it in Eden. No doubt a computer program exists these days which could take us on a walk through the town as envisioned by Charlie Frazier, including the 1000 paper lots the Seashore deprived him of his right to develop in the pursuit of profits and his vision of a bigger and better Wellfleet.

You might think the shadow of the Original Sin would fall heavily on the recent DCPC uproar, but it doesn't seem to have made us any less suspicious of even a hint of outside interference or less confident demanding local self-determination than we were 40 years ago.

It would be fitting to observe the 40th by a townwide mock referendum (with, say, a month's notice for reflection and debate). Question: If the federal government were to give us the vote we didn't get 40 years ago to determine whether we want to go on living in

Eden or cash it in (not such a stretch under Dubya, who would like to return as much public land as possible to private companies for profitable. exploitation) how would you vote?

There has been for a long time the impression that however it felt 40 years ago, Outer Capers strongly support the Seashore, despite occasional squabbles over details of management. It would be fascinating to find out the reality. Of course a mock vote wouldn't necessarily approximate the results of a real and binding referendum; it's easy enough to pay lip service to the Seashore when there is no real possibility of making money from developing it.

I know people even in this enlightened town who think we all have the right to eat that apple, whatever the consequences. There may be more such folks in town than we think.

MAKING AN HONEST
DUMP OUT OF US

LET'S TALK TRASH. Here in Wellfleet, gem of the Outer Cape, we still refer to the place where we take our garbage as The Dump. Dump, a sort of reverse euphemism, has a more honest sound to it than Transfer Station, even though using the traditional term dishonestly skirts the reality that for the past decade or more, what we deposit only perches there awaiting transference to some else's town off-Cape, where what we mean by the term dumping actually takes place.

I have been scavenging around for the date of the first centralized, public dump in our town. There are at least two major stages in our alienation from our garbage. The most recent started in 1988 when the dump became a transfer station, making that useful modern concept of NIMBY (not in my backyard) official town trash philosophy.

But the first application of NIMBY was when we as a town decided it was no longer OK to burn or bury our stuff in our individual backyards and set aside public land as central dumping ground. That date would seem just as significant as marking the end of an era as the switch to transfer station. But no one seems to know just when that was. I called the DPW and the dump itself and asked to speak to their resident historians, but it turns out we have never budgeted such positions. Judy Stetson's standard 1963 history of our town is a little weak on the trash part of that history and doesn't mention the momentous occasion.

One friend who has been around since the '40s says the dump was there when he arrived. Another old-timer says that around 1930 there was dumping on Brown's Neck Road about a half-mile from the present dump, although he didn't know whether that was a town-sanctioned site or just sufficiently nobody's backyard at the time to suggest itself as a logical repository. It is logical to think that the switch to central dumping had something to do with the advent of plastics and other high tech stuff too smelly to burn and with too long a half-life to bury. But that would put the date post-WWII, usually cited as the start to the proliferation of plastics.

Selectman Roger Putnam is pushing the composting and recycling system run by Waste Options Inc. to great advantage on Nantucket (where practicing NIMBY by ferrying off the local product would be especially costly). This system has several advantages, we are told, including saving money over the present practice of trucking off-Cape and producing compost to augment our anemic local topsoil.

Another advantage of composting our own garbage is that it would put some reality behind our preference for the honest sound of the term Dump. It would once again make an honest dump out of us.

JEKYLL AND HYDE

THERE IS A SORT OF SPLIT personality built into this newspaper. The front news section often carries stories about problems of crowding and overdevelopment— traffic jams, the crisis in affordable housing, the struggle to save open space. Meanwhile, the business section features stories with a whole different slant: stories applauding upturns in hotel reservations or the boom in new construction, much of it second homes; or lamenting the opposite. It's as if the two parts of the paper, like Jekyll and Hyde (not to say which is which), inhabit two different worlds.

On May 8, for instance, as tourist season approached and Section A began to feature letters and stories on seasonal gridlock on the bridges, the business section headline lamented in large letters: "The numbers are in and they're not pretty; Cape spending down in first quarter, says economic report." One of the prime indicators of a "problem" cited was a decline in the traffic over the bridges.

Say what? Given the front-section stories, why would the writer of this story imagine that a decline in the tourist trade would be thought of as a problem? The answer, of course, is not editorial confusion about the nature of the paper's audience. The split between the two parts of the paper reflects the reality that we, the readership, are indeed split. There is the business community—including all those in the business of renting out their homes seasonally—that suffers when tourist numbers are down. And then there are the rest of us who suffer when the tourist numbers are up.

But that split is simplistic. If the paper seems schizoid, that reflects not only a diverse Cape constituency, but a contradiction within many individual readers. There is the part of us—carpenter, waitress, realtor, seasonal landlord—that rejoices at an article about booming tourism or housing starts (gleefully reaping in advance fat tips, still higher rents); and there is the part of us that would really rather not see those same people at the pond, the restaurant, making life more stressful on Route 6 or in the aisles at the supermarket.

There is the part of our life in which we profit from tourists . . . and the other part which profits from lack of tourists.

Going back to the May 8 story on the decline of tourist numbers, the article cites problems in the national economy as the likely reason. But could it be that tourists have begun to read the first section of the paper about the various problems created by our popularity and consequent love/hate relationship with visitors and have, the more sensitive ones, decided to stay away? Reading front-section stories might well give tourists the idea they would be doing us a big favor to stay away. On the other hand, reading the biz section, they might get to feeling guilty about staying home or deciding to grace some other vacation venue. (Hey honey, maybe we should change our mind about the Maine vacation. Says here Cape tourist numbers are down and they're hurting. They need us.)

It would be a good guess that a lot of us who have chosen to live here full-time would never have taken our first vacation to this Cape. The very thing that made us come as tourists originally was peace and quiet and simplicity. What makes us stay on full-time as washashores or natives (aside from the fact that it is home) is that much of the year this still is——I can vouch for the Outer Cape anyway—a very quiet, away-from-it-all sort of place. It is hard to understand people who would on their vacations deliberately subject themselves to what we have become in the summer. I have the feeling that those of us who were attracted to the Cape of 20 or 30 years ago would take one look at this Cape and keep on driving.

I must say, now that summer is here, it's hard to see what that May 8 story was talking about; the numbers of tourists certainly don't seem down. But I wouldn't blame tourists for wising up and going someplace less fraught, someplace that could give them now what we used to provide. And while the part of us who live on tourist numbers might lament the decline in profits, the other part might take comfort in the other sort of profit, the sort we came here for originally.

THE LITTLE PHARM THAT APPARENTLY COULDN'T

HOW OFTEN DOES THE CLOSING of a small-town drugstore make the front page of a newspaper emanating from a city 30 miles away? In this case it is the very insignificance of the Wellfleet Pharmacy that makes it front page material. It's only a podunk drugstore. Another one bites the dust. . . .

I recently learned that the corporate pharmaceutical form of globalization is called Big Pharma. The Wellfleet store was Little Pharma, Main Street, small-town, I-think-I-can Pharma. And it's gone. It thought it could, we all hoped it could, but turned out it couldn't. Or didn't want to. Or something. The cause of death is not quite clear yet. Results of autopsy pending.

In this region called Cape Cod the Wellfleet Pharmacy is meaningful beyond its size because it is one of the few remaining functions of one of the very few towns that at least look and feel like a link to the past that so defines our present.

The romance of small town is powerful. Until fairly recently, like others, I thought of this town as more or less intact. I wanted to think of it as a conduit to the past, a genuine holdover from another era. I wanted—I needed—the connection. When we—actually the Chamber, I suppose—started calling Wellfleet the Gallery

Town, it seemed like wishful thinking. Sure, we had some fine art for sale in our town; but the reason we had long been the sort of place artists like to live is, paradoxically, that we were the sort of scruffy, real town that would never become so tamed and gentrified as to actually become a Gallery Town. I was happy when people from other parts of the Cape would call Wellfleet one of the very last old-fashioned towns left.

But of course that isn't true. The town we were looks like it's still here, but it isn't. As with many another former town, most of our Main Street of 50 years ago is to be found scattered in one up-Cape mall or another. We are more ghost town than not.

The pharmacy is perhaps the cruelest cut of all from the Main Street lineup—a service of life-and-death importance with a personalized, local flavor just not available in CVS.

A big part of the story of the pharmacy closing is the hurt bewilderment of its former patrons: But we depended on the pharmacy, we patronized it. How could it not have been a good business? Apparently, the owner's family situation was part of the picture: the pharmacist, sister of the owner, needs to move away because her husband got a job elsewhere. But the owner is also quoted alluding to the difficulty of attracting a new pharmacist to such a small operation.

So maybe this latest in a series of closings is, along with the forced erection of cell phone antennas, just the tide of globalization we have been reading about finally reaching this shore?

Only six years ago this town approved in Town Meeting a Comprehensive Plan with an optimistic vision of a revitalized year-round downtown. There seemed in this document no question we could have the town we wanted if we got clear about it and put it down in writing. But a short time ago I was sitting around with a group of more-active-than-average citizens (a couple of them, I believe, members of the committee that drafted the Comprehensive Plan) discussing recent closings and rumors of closings. And everyone seemed agreed that there really was nothing to be done about the town coming apart at the seams. If we couldn't support a pharmacy or a grocery store that could eliminate the need for trips to big box stores in Orleans, that was just the way things are in our times. Small and local must, by iron laws of economics, eventually succumb to huge and global. The closings must mean that it just isn't good business any more to have a functioning town here.

Given this fatalism on the part of devoted locals the optimism of the Comprehensive Plan begins to look more like an historical artifact than a believable, hopeful plan of action.

We are used to leaving business to businessmen and the laws of supply and demand. The owner of the pharmacy space is reportedly looking for another pharmacy to replace the defunct one. But maybe the time has come for us, as a community, to begin to advertise our need. WANTED: pharmacist to play important role in small town. Any shortcomings in salary more than compensated by you and your family becoming part of the fabric of a genuine community.

EQUAL ACCESS
AND
THE TOILET ANALOGY

EARLY MORNING RUN to the Wellfleet Cumby's for emergency halfnhalf. Standing with a fellow citizen marvelling at a surprisingly energized Route 6—7:30 and already a steady stream of traffic. Can't all be locals making their way to jobs. Must be up-and-at-'em tourists propelled by all that enterprise which made them the money which buys them a piece of us for a week or two.

We get into lamenting the crowding of life here in summer. He brings up the old idea of a big sign on the other side of the canal: CAPE COD FULL. NEXT AVAILABLE SPACE IN APPROXIMATELY X MINUTES. TAKE A NUMBER. This joke, full of attitude toward the summer invasion, has been around for a couple of decades at least. These days it might get serious consideration in some quarters: Hmmm . . . you know . . .

Promenading down Commercial Street in Provincetown the summer crowd seems a rich swarm of life, the scene we go there to become part of, melt into. But the nonstop traffic on Route 6, probably a lot of the same folks heading for Commercial Street, has a whole different feel and meaning. Instead of a groovy flow, more like the Cape about to have a stroke.

But despite a lot of grousing about the congestion we are doing our best to pack them in. And the thinking is in place to support the idea that indeed everyone has an equal right to the natural wonders of the Outer Cape. The idea of declaring the Cape to be full and making people wait on the other side of the canal for a space seems downright un-democratic.

A former Wellfleet selectman wrote a letter back in June to the editor of the *Cape Cod Times* criticizing a local couple opposed to the town meeting article re-grandfathering certain undersized lots. "Why would they deny to others what they and their family enjoy? Surely they have no monopoly on the appreciation of Wellfleet's natural beauty."

I imagined as I read this a lot of readers nodding their heads in agreement, no matter what they might otherwise think about the undersized lots issue. It goes against the American grain to deny access to others: What makes you think you're better than anyone else? Shouldn't everyone get a shot at our natural assets? The National Seashore declared this a "national treasure" 40 years ago; wasn't that just another way of yelling, "Come and get it"? Our duty, it follows, is to enhance accessibility by all means possible: more and faster ferries, straighter, wider roads, the Sagamore rotary flyover now being discussed.

And of course no one does have a special entitlement to live in this or any other nice place on earth. But if not everyone who might like to can fit in a particular place such as this without ruining it for everyone, which seems to be the case, who should decide when enough is enough, when the reasonable limit has been reached? God? The stock market? The building industry?

No—of available choices, local citizens, having the biggest stake, should have the responsibility (and yes, the right—the two usually go together). Not because we are special cases, morally superior, inherently more deserving, but only because we ended up here—made the choice to leave other places and commit to this one. Because we are here and in position to know the place and make decisions about its needs. Because residency entails the responsibility of stewardship. (Unfortunately, we who live here are also well placed to profit from crowding and that's a complicating factor.)

We seem to understand, when it comes to a public toilet, that if we didn't wait in line there would be unfortunate consequences and no one would get to use it. When it comes to restaurants the logic is clear: if people started sitting on each others' laps, eating on the floor, the experience we seek in a restaurant would be spoiled. So we submit our hunger to reservations or first come, first served, both governed by the actual limits of the space.

Maybe a vast parking lot on the other side of the bridge for those waiting for their turn on Cape Cod is not the answer. But we do need an answer. (The "Outer Cape Capacity Study" of a few years ago predicted that by 2020 January traffic would resemble that of today's summer unless ways are found of limiting development.) One place to start is to banish from our discussions the fallacy that limiting development and crowding has anything to do with class privilege or exclusivity.

WELLFLEET
AND THE WORLD:
A 9/11 MEDLEY

LATE IN THE AFTERNOON of Tuesday, September
11, I walked over to the pond. I came upon it in an
especially peaceful moment, one of those moods when
the pond seem most pond-like—reflecting the pines and a
few soft clouds drifting in the blue sky, registering the
occasional ghost of a breeze; but otherwise quiet, self-
absorbed, a little world unto itself, innocent of the
booming surf only a mile away. Innocent of the events of
the day.

And here I was, at the pond, then in the pond—surely
I could share in its innocence and disconnection? The
Outer Cape has always been about disconnection. A
move here, a geographical removal, is also an emotional
withdrawal, in part from those crowded centers of
population, those very symbols of affluence that came
most sickeningly tumbling down. But I couldn't help but
imagine, even while bathing in the pond's innocence,
being on those planes, heading for those buildings, the
minutes in those buildings before the towers collapsed in
that image they kept running on TV again and again like a
screen-saver.

If I still lived in my childhood home north of The
City, my mind ran on, I would probably know a lot of
people in those buildings. Kim once had an office in the

tower right where the plane hit. Wait a minute…where does Irene work? God, Logan…it could have been us getting on one of those planes.

We compulsively try to connect with this history happening not very far away. Run to the blood bank, get our blood into the ones who were there in that history. Stay glued to the TV images as those towers flame and crumble over and over. And we hope there is no connection, in the form of friends caught in that history. Six degrees of separation is not very many with that many victims.

Am I here? Or there, with those nightmarishly collapsing towers?

Be here now, says the pond.

Be there, says the mind.

ω ω ω

ONE EFFECT OF THE SHOCK of September 11 may be to deepen our understanding of the meaning of so-called skyscrapers.

In an article recently printed in these pages Benjamin Forgey argued that precisely because tall buildings stand as "prideful" symbols of U.S. power, it is necessary for us to reassert ourselves by rebuilding on the World Trade Center site something equally big and prideful. A sort of skyscraper version of getting back on the horse is what he seems to have in mind. In an accompanying piece, Roger Ebert argued that we should not rebuild but instead cultivate the site as a green field, a comforting piece of the "earth that we share."

There is an echo in this disagreement of the local Cape Cod struggle between those who wish to erect structures on still vacant land and those who want to see it bought up by towns aided by the land bank and preserved as open space. It is not too far fetched to think of skyscrapers as trophy buildings—the architecture of hubris.

Growing up in the suburbs north of The City, as it likes to think of itself, I was taken into Manhattan on birthdays and other special occasions. One of the most impressive parts of those trips was the experience of simply looking up. Awe probably comes closest to explaining that experience of craning one's neck in the canyons of Manhattan, an awe consisting in an inability to comprehend, to encompass the looming immensity of those buildings New York is famous for.

Another way of putting this is to say that there is indeed, in this experience of awe, something awful about such buildings. Something oppressive as well as impressive. With these trophy buildings you give up the comfort of human scale for the very different sort of comfort of identifying with power and affluence, the stability and invincibility of the social and political whole.

More famous (as well as, QED, more durable) than the World Trade Center are the great pyramids of Egypt. Perhaps because these Wonders of the World have outlived the political regimes that produced them, their full meaning is part of our shared understanding of them. We know about the thousands of slaves who gave their lives in one way or another in their construction; we know about the authoritarian political and social order needed to produce these monuments. I haven't seen a poll on the subject, but I imagine many of us might feel that the Wonder is not worth the price that was paid. The WTC was, by contrast, produced by construction workers out of free choice, as we define freedom in our economic system. But lot of human life, as well as an enormous amount of other resources, went into that building, too.

Perhaps it is a comfort to feel a part of a civilization that can produce such wonders of the world as the WTC; maybe it's worth all the human hours, sweat, resources that went into building it. Maybe it's even worth the risk—as it went up there were those who publicly spoke of the risk—that it can be knocked down.

There is also something to be said for the comforts of the human scaled villages of Cape Cod. In our town 28 feet up is as high as code allows you to go, a problem the trophy house impulse must exercise ingenuity in circumventing. Behind the code is the value that no structure should dominate the landscape or others' views of the landscape. Our typical buildings are low, built of relatively soft materials, big enough to house a family, yet not so big as to overawe. Definitely on the unmonumental, unprideful side. Ground-hugging is more the instinct around here than skyscraping.

As one whom skyscrapers have inspired with awe and who has enjoyed the bird's eye view from the top, I nevertheless vote with Ebert on the subject of what to do with Ground Zero: not necessarily a field but, if a building, one with a little less awe, a little less pride—at least that sort of pride. Not out of fear so much as a sense that architecture is capable of expressing more profound and humanly nourishing values than awe and pride.

Maybe we are seeing the end of a stage we went through of constructing trophy buildings; and maybe that would not be such a bad thing.

ω ω ω

A BIG PIECE OF THE LOGIC OF LIFE on the Outer Cape is our isolationism. For most of our history it's been a big world in which we were happy to be a small place, well separated from other places. So the idea that "it's a small world," despite its cozy sound, would seem to go against the local grain. The agenda of globalization, whether forcing us onto the cell phone grid or making us a part of the international Stop & Shop food family threatens the very nature of this place.

On Sept. ll, when the headquarters of globalization got globalized back with a vengeance, our hearts and telephone calls went out to those lived close to Ground Zero. We watched our share of TV coverage and felt part of the nation, the "we" that had been attacked. But on the other hand, it didn't seem likely that anytime soon terrorists would be directing hijacked planes at the Pilgrim Monument or Wellfleet Congo church steeple.

But then came the stories about anthrax—if they can mail that powder anywhere they can mail it here too. Suddenly friends down at the P.O. seemed more part of the nation under attack than the rest of us. (I realize that at this point it's not at all certain that the anthrax scare is being brought to us by the same network who brought us Sept. ll.). Then the idea of someone deliberately infected with smallpox walking into a crowd. Sure, that would probably mean a city; but unlike anthrax smallpox is highly infectious. That could very quickly whittle down the six degrees to no degrees at all.

I happened to tune into a guy on NPR who seemed to know what he was talking about going on about how just about anybody can download a do-it-yourself kit, get a hold of a tiny amount of the fissionable material that it turns out is easier to score these days than cocaine, and voila: a nuclear weapon of your very own to be delivered a la Tim McVeigh. It's no longer just a couple of so-called rogue nations we've got to worry about—it's anybody with Sept. ll-style ambitions to wreak havoc.

Even more upclose-and-personal, the stories on the vulnerability of the local nuclear power plant. That threat is only a half hour away as the prevailing winds would waft a cloud of radiactive dust. We should all have our supply of potassium iodide pills against radiation sickness, says a *Cape Cod Times* editorial.

A lot of the challenge to Outer Cape isolationism is just conjecture at the moment, mostly newspaper articles. Stop & Shop coming to Truro seems a more real threat.

But I haven't been feeling of late quite as isolated as I'd like.

In a sense, I've always been an isolationist. In 17 years living in Hartford I never once took a walk in the North End, which was widely perceived to be so poor as to make even a modestly well-off person a target. When I visited NYC, I did not hang out in Harlem or the Bronx. I did not choose to subject myself to the conditions in which many of my fellow citizens are mired.

A couple of weeks ago the *New York Times* magazine ran an article on the grinding poverty and hopeless, debilitating work that is the lot of boys and young men in Peshawar, Pakistan. When I read that sort of thing a year ago I would deplore it, but a part of the experience of reading was that the misery of those lives was there, I was here. If, living in Hartford, I didn't have to subject myself to the reality of most of my fellow citizens, I certainly didn't have to subject myself to the realities of Peshawar. If I took a vacation it would not be to tour that misery. But the point of this article was that I might not have to. The condition of these young men's lives made them likely terrorists; they might be exporting their misery in the form of anthrax, smallpox, suitcase nukes.

It's a 911 aftermath cliche to say it's a whole new world, but we don't really know what this new world looks like now that we are in it. It's hard to know how scared it is reasonable to be. For every expert that warns that we better get used to an insecure future, there is another who says get a grip, we've got these terrorists on the run, we have nothing to fear but fear itself.

Something is happening but we don't know what it is, do we, Mr. Jones?

What if this is what's happening: that every poorest, most desperate, nothing-to-lose third world erstwhile victim of globalization (or lack thereof, depending on your perspective) now has his finger on the red nuke'em button formerly reserved for the heads of state of the major cold war powers? That anybody in the world can now kill everybody in the world. How's that for one big happy family? May be an exaggeration, but an exaggeration with a kernel of truth about the world that was born on 911.

It's this Cape isolationist's worst nightmare (and stuff of many a scary Hollywood moment): finding yourself in the wrong side of town. Being subject to the miseries of others in the human family.

WABI-SABI

WHY AM I ALWAYS THE LAST on my block to know about cutting-edge trends? The latest *Utne Reader* (digest of alternative periodicals) brings the news that the mainland is all agog with something called wabi-sabi. Turns out feng shui, which I was just getting comfortable with, is yesterday's unpronounceable eastern concept. (Feng shui is designing your house for an optimal spiritual influence and a mighty handy thing it is, too, keeping you from locating your bed too near the furnace, and so on.)

Now, says *Utne*, the thing is wabi-sabi. Everybody across the bridge is talking about it and improving themselves with it. In the spirituality department we Outer Capers are, as is too often the case, already lagging far behind.

About now you may be muttering to yourself, "What the heck is he talking about?" Here's a quote from *Utne*: "Wabi-sabi is the Japanese tradition of celebrating the beauty in what's flawed or worn. It offers an inspiring new way to look at your home, and your whole life. … Wabi-sabi is everything that today's sleek, mass-produced, technology-saturated culture isn't. It's flea markets, not shopping malls …Wabi-sabi understands the tender, raw beauty of a gray December landscape and the aching elegance of an abandoned building or shed. It celebrates the cracks and crevices and rot and all the other marks that time and weather and use leave behind."

From which I gather that wabi-sabi is a sort of retreat position: if you have failed to employ feng shui to perfect your house, you bring in the wabi-sabi to make yourself feel better at having to live in it anyway.

What wabi-sabi seems to come down to in mainland America, where there is a spanking new Stop & Shop or Walmart every 50 feet or so, is the fetish we have had for the past decade or two for tokens of a more soulful way we used to be—such as overpriced, half-wornout denim items and deliberately banged-up old bureaus with layers of old paint showing through. Except imperfect things like that don't count, according to the article. In fact, consumer fetishes are the spiritual opposite of wabi-sabi.

A few years ago I wrote a column or two trying to get at the essence of the charm of Outer Cape towns like Wellfleet, as compared with more kempt, spiffy, competent places up-Cape. I used words like "eyesores, flaking, rotting, decaying, hodgepodge" to describe parts of us. I meant this fondly, but as I found out afterwards, some readers thought I was insulting our town. Well, as we drift inexorably toward what we hope we will be in the mood to appreciate as the raw beauty of the gray December landscape, I am happy to be able to say that this wabi-sabi concept seems to be exactly what I was trying to get at. "Aching elegance" may be a bit over the top, but abandoned buildings and sheds—definitely. And what town landmark celebrates cracks and crevices more than Uncle Tim's? (Well, maybe Truro's town hall.) Let's face it, Wellfleet is a wabi-sabi town. Filled with a lot of wabi-sabi people, too. Charming not despite but because of our imperfections.

In fact, the only real imperfections for many of us are, paradoxically, such attempts to improve and perfect as the transfer station, which definitely has less wabi-sabi than the dump, which is why most of us go on using the old term. The new DPW and police/fire station, I'm afraid, have little of the wabi of their predecessors (the premature decay of the latter doesn't count as wabi, only as incompetence). Tourist-oriented stores named "I Used to be a Pickle" have less of it than the traditional, useful pharmacy we just lost.

I feel a lot better to have come across a highly approved, genuine eastern concept to lend retroactive legitimacy to my characterization of this town.

Once we get clear that wabi-sabi is what the Outer Cape is all about, charting our future course becomes much easier. The threatened Stop & Shop, precisely because of all its many virtues, is not wabi-sabi. A wabi-sabi attitude toward Wellfleet's traditionally imperfect but tasty and chlorine-free water would go a long way toward saving us a lot of money, disruption, and the chemical tinkering that inevitably comes with public water systems.

Now that we know how the denizens of suburbia/urbia hunger for it, the selectmen would do well to feature wabi-sabi on the new town website (recognizing, of course, that a website itself is profoundly un-wabi). Wellfleet, the wabi-sabi town.

LIVING WITH SAND ROADS

THERE ARE CERTAIN THINGS about this town which might look to an outsider dysfunctional but which, on closer observation, prove otherwise. Like, for instance, our many sand roads.

At this point, three quarters of a century or so into the almost universal conversion to pavement, you would have to say that these roads are more than the result of inadvertence; we seem to prefer them. In fact, to judge from my own sand road neighborhood, most of the many citizens who live with sand roads everyday would attack with bazookas any town machines sent to pave them. Sand roads are as much a part of local character as the ponds they often lead to, the older houses and cottages, the working boat hulls left to rot at the edges of our harbor.

Despite what seems clear citizen preference, our official town policy is road surface competence. All new developments of any size are required to feature not only paved roads, but wide paved roads: 20 feet wide, with artificial landscaping another 10 feet on either side. This requirement, as much as the stripping of indigenous ground cover and clear-cutting of trees, is a reason new neighborhoods look like they were flown in from suburban New Jersey or Ohio and deposited here.

Our ever-zealous DPW keeps trying to nudge existing sand roads toward hard surfaced respectability by importing alien materials such as sand made yellowish by clay content (the usual color is whitish, which makes it easy to follow on foot with even a hint of moonlight). Grey crushed stone and stone dust are also used, which does a good job of hardening the contours of any potholes. Once they spread stuff the length of our road which turned out to contain chunks of rebar, rusty wire, and other kinds of shrapnel—for better traction, I suppose. We are still picking up pieces years later.

On the Outer Cape, as elsewhere, the hardening of roads tracked the advent of the automobile. They were first oiled, in the 'teens, then blacktopped in the 20s. It does seem a logical thing to do: make a road smoother, faster, easier on car and driver. Why then did this town, unlike most, stop well short of universal pavement? Why not just pave 'em all and be done with it? Clearly, at some point we just grew fond of the qualities of sand roads.

Sand roads are soft and sinuous, following the contours of the land, unlike most paved roads that abtractly slice through it. Being narrow, usually one car's width, they are integrated into the landscape, barely parting the forest they run through. Nature presses in on both sides as one penetrates the woods on way to pond or home. A sand road feels like a refuge, as if, when you leave the pavement behind, you are already home, going down your own driveway. You have submitted to the spirit of the local place.

Sand roads don't require speed bumps. And while being forced to slow way down sounds like a big inconvenience, it doesn't usually feel that way. It is nice to feel like less of a threat to other forms of life; your comfortable pace sets you less apart from walkers, makes it easier to greet them, separates you less from the reality that you, too, are a walker some of the time.

Wait a minute, you say, back up: did you say one car's width? That's all nice and romantic . . . but what happens when two cars meet? You don't mean to say one has to actually back up to a point where it can pull off to let the other pass? Who decides who backs up? Must be a sticky situation, road rage waiting to happen. Talk about dysfunctional.

Actually, the occasional head-on meeting of two cars in the woods is, most of the time, less a nuisance than a moment of ritual connection with a neighbor. It's true, an "after you, Alphonse" sort of confusion wouldn't do. The routine is that the minute you see a car ahead, both parties make instant calculations as to how far past a driveway or other such widening each has travelled and act accordingly. If I know that I passed a driveway 50 feet back and you passed one 100 feet back, without hesitation I begin to back up while you wait . . . and vice versa. The wave exchanged in passing is less "thanks" than "hi" and mutual appreciation of this moment of living with our good old sand road, of how well we have handled it.

The Ritual of the Pass requires of both parties precise, intimate, almost pre-conscious knowledge of the road. When you run into a summer renter you often sense confusion, sometimes a note of suburban/urban confrontation: their car suggesting by its body language that your car should now start backing, simply because it's in their way, even if they have just passed a driveway. You, possessed of local knowledge, know that you would have to back 150 feet to let them by, hold your ground, hoping by your refusal to accommodate them—and maybe some gesturing through the windshield—to teach them the reasonable thing. But when they finally do take the hint, the back-up is often done awkwardly, with attitude: you did this to them—you in your non-BMW conspiring with this annoyingly incompetent road.

But such occasional unpleasantness is the exception that proves the rule. And even then there is smug satisfaction

—you know how to do this dance, even if this particular partner is a klutz.

ω ω ω

[*one month later . . .*]

AS IF BY WAY OF ILLUSTRATION of my contention in a recent column that citizen fondness for soft-surfaced roads and official town road policy may conflict, our DPW earlier this week decided to widen the swath my own neighborhood's road makes through the woods by cutting back brush and small trees for a few feet on both sides. This was, in the view of the DPW, a mere trim, a minor cosmetic alteration, and yet neighbors came out of the woodwork to make life difficult for those responsible for what felt like an assault on the neighborhood's quality of life.

The destruction of familiar plant life aside, the main fear about widening the swath of the road is that if drivers are no longer paying a price in a scratched paint job, they will feel encouraged to pass and the one-lane road will become a two lane road. This will in turn make it faster, destroying a vital part of its charm and logic.

People lamented the wanton mangling of a favorite little tree or bush. One man, reminding himself of a 'sixties style protestor, stepped in front of a large machine to prevent its progress past his house. Irate calls were made to selectmen and the Town Administrator.

Rousted out by a call from a neighbor on the front line, I wandered down to see what the fuss was about and got into an interesting conversation with the assistant DPW director, who was hoping for a sympathetic ear. It went something like the following:

Jeez, I can't believe that guy up the road throwing himself into the path of our equipment. Actually accused me of taking a bribe to do this. Unbelievable.

Well, as you now see, people care a lot about these sand roads. By the way, how did the decision get made to come and remodel our roadway?

Fire trucks and road maintenance trucks can't get down the road because it's too narrow.

But they've been getting down up until now. What's changed?

We've got this new truck and its paint is getting scratched.

And that's the reason you are cutting back the forest?

Well, it's your truck, paid for by your taxes, don't you care about the paint job?

Not as much as we care about this road. Why not get a smaller truck more suited to this kind of work? There are a lot of sand roads in this town.

In case you haven't noticed, trucks are getting bigger.

You mean there are no small trucks?

Well, we aren't buying them.

If we had known when the purchase of the big truck came up in Town Meeting that it would create this problem, citizens might have asked you look around until you found a smaller truck, one that fits the road you've got to work with. Maybe a used one with the paint already scratched to avoid that new truck trauma.

Hey, I'm just trying to do my job, he said plaintively; and you could see that he was. He just couldn't understand the people of this town getting so het up about cutting back a little brush for heaven's sake . . . And now he had to get back to work; you could see that all this talking about the aesthetics of sand roads was not, as far as he was concerned, part of the job description.

It was a moment of rare clarity. The town in its DPW mode seeing its clear duty to protect the paint job of the people's property. The town in the form of residents seeing the truck, our own truck, and its needs as a threat against our roadway, against our quality of life.

But the plot thickened. Seems the request to beat back nature on this particular road might have come from the police department responding to a complaint. A part-time resident had trouble getting a fat boat down this narrow road and wanted it widened to accommodate his recreational needs. One call from one non-resident and the DPW jumps into action. No attempt to find out how residents might feel about the idea of enlarging the roadway. (You could appreciate how the boat guy's need and the worries about that vulnerable paint job would look to the DPW like the proverbial two birds.)

By the time I wandered back up the road to my house, a selectman had driven over to view the carnage. The DPW had been asked to withdraw their forces for the time being (driving off with collective shaking of heads). The issue will be on the agenda of the next meeting of the selectmen, who will be asked to sort out the needs of trucks vs. the needs of people.

Meanwhile, the assistant DPW director, who lives, in the way of this new era, in another town, has yet another story to tell about the strange people he works for.

VARIETIES OF
POND POLLUTION

I WAS PRIVY a couple of weeks ago to a ten minute cell phone chat a woman had with a business associate in the late morning of a dropdead gorgeous day at Dyer Pond. I gathered the business had to do with a getting a contract signed. The tone was friendly but businesslike. The person at the other end, in an office somewhere, was apparently performing according to my pondmate's satisfaction. Things were well in hand. She would check in again soon.

How do I know the intimate details of this woman's business? Lying on my cloth 150 yards down the sandy margin I could not help but hear it. On a breathless morning at the pond, sound broadcasts with amazing clarity. Like the couple of other parties pondside, I was made a captive audience.

It's finally happened, the scenario the anti-cell phone locals warned against several years ago when the cell phone companies came to persuade us to cooperate with the cell phone revolution: somebody at the pond who is not really at the pond. Cell phone conversation sounds different from conversation with someone actually present. It sounds like you are not there. It's a sound that pollutes and dilutes this place with the caller's connection to another place.

This is probably not the first time a cell phone has been used from pondside, only the first time I've been there to witness it. But I'm enough of a habitue to have a sense that in a world that has been inundated by the cell phone universal accessibility, our ponds have been deliberately preserved as cell phone-free zones. It is part of the implicit code of conduct at these ponds not to use it. This woman was committing a breach of pond etiquette.

This unwritten code was in place for decades before the cell phone era. It governs with some precision, for instance, how close one party arriving at the pond should get to another party already ensconced there. You don't bring a boombox. At least until a certain hour (or unless you are a clueless teenager) you don't express your joy at coming upon such a pristine setting by large yelps and yahoos; quiet appreciation is more the mode called for. You don't wash your hair there, or water your dog. You don't drive your SUV to the edge of the pond for convenience and wouldn't even if there were not a Seashore chain across the road five minutes away. You appreciate that relative inaccessibility, whether by cars or telephones, is the essence of its charm.

All this is in striking contrast with the implicit code of the public corner of Long Pond less than a ten-minute walk away. There, at least once the early morning esthetes have returned home for their coffee, cheek-by-jowl is the rule. Driving as close as possible and unloading as much play gear as possible is cool. Public displays of glee are not frowned upon. It's a young family scene, and probably most families, locals and summerfolk, who come here over the years at some point find it the indispensable mode of enjoying a pond.

I hope all this agreeable togetherness doesn't include the joys of sharing urine. A couple of years ago I emerged from a quicky swim at Long Pond to see a senior woman fondly cheering on her three year old grandson as he peed in the very water now dripping from my body.

To my pointed objection—Hey, I was just swimming in that water—she amiably replied: Oh but it is such a large pond (surely large enough to subsume the bladder contents of many children). But, but... It was clear we were operating out of two very different pond universes. I surrendered the field, her genuine perplexity at my not wanting to swim in her grandchild's pee leaving me wondering whether the Long Pond code now does in fact include not only the inevitability, as always in such a family setting, but the actual acceptability of toddler pee.

At Dyer, a world away, as I lay there on my blanket listening to the cell phone woman chirping away I considered stopping off on my out to let her know she was committing a faux pas; did she really want the whole pond to know her business? But when it comes to playing enforcer of a point of pond etiquette, more often than not I decide that getting into it with the offender is another form of pollution, probably even more unpleasant. And yet, I argued with myself, isn't it a duty of a longtime friend of Dyer to let her know? Maybe she's new, doesn't know the code and would fall all over herself with gratitude, like the person clued in about his bad breath in the old advertisement (Oh my goodness, I had no idea. Really? Thanks ever so.) More likely it would go: Get lost, nature nazi. It's a free country isn't it? What's wrong with accessibility anyway? How great you can sit cooling your tootsies in this beautiful water and taking a meeting at the same time.

So I just left, assuaging my inner conflict with the comforting thought that I might just have to write a column about this (although that particular cell phone perpetrator is probably long gone back to paying full attention to business).

THE AESTHETICS
OF SHELLFISHING

"SHELLFISH FARMERS CAN USE TIDAL FLATS" read a headline back in July reporting the legal victory of three Wellfleet aquaculturists in their seven year struggle with a retired North Carolina executive who has been trying to prevent them from plying their ancient trade in front of his waterfront property. The exec plans to appeal.

What does this issue mean to an ignorant bystander? I don't know cultch from a clutch and as far as I'm concerned spat is the past tense of expectorate. My closest brush with shellfishing was being part of a boisterous party of amateur and probably illegal clamdiggers scrounging for ingredients for a vat of chowder for a houseful back in the mid-'70s. But there are some issues here that seem to me to be of importance even to those of us who neither get our shoes muddy on a regular basis nor own million dollar waterfront. Like the movement to give non-residents the vote and the purge of our neighborhoods a few years back of the appearance that workers live in this town, the very fact that this aesthetics vs. use conflict is coming up at all seems a troubling sign of the times

Beyond the legal hairsplitting, is our harbor there for use by the public, including shellfish grants, or is it there to serve as a view from the deck of the fortunate owner of upland property? The quick answer, I guess, is it depends on whether you are a waterfront owner or a flats worker.

Until recently the answer would have been: both. When exactly did tidal flats workers start being seen as spoiling the view? A lot of us might not be thrilled at the sight of workers erecting a cell phone tower forced on us by the industry; some of us would not warm to the sight of construction workers building the controversial Truro Stop & Shop should that come to pass. I'm not at all sure I would want the view from my house to include a soda ash and industrial phosphate factory (that's how the North Carolina retired executive made his money). But it seems to me there used to be postcards featuring old-time Codders doing old-time Cape sorts of things—fishing, repairing nets, cutting up a pod of blackfish washed up on the beach. I have a print of a Winslow Homer painting of a New England scene featuring two young men carrying up the beach a big bucket of something—most likely shellfish. He could easily have left these two young workers out; I have to think he considered them a picturesque part of a picturesque scene. But now apparently the flats workers are flies in the ointment of this executive's view.

It seems to all come down to the meaning of the activity in question. I have to admit that I have always found the murmur of guys and their pickups a couple of hundred yards out on the flats of an autumn or winter dusk to be part of the pleasure of a walk along the harbor. It probably isn't picturesque to them (although I've heard some say that just being out there is a perk of the job); but it's picturesque to me. Reminds me of Millet's paintings of field workers. And yes, sure, that's just a romantic picture, but no doubt part of my finding it picturesque is that I like the idea of fellow townspeople making their living that way, in the same way that I like the smell of the sea breeze, the way the old houses look, other ways that we are and have been for a long time. (But then—full disclosure—I know a lot more shellfishermen than wealthy waterfront owners.)

Houses still look the way they did 100 or 200 years ago but the life led in them is completely different. But these harbor harvesters are, although in an updated way, actually doing the same things as generations of Wellfleetians. I wouldn't regard this activity as a pollution of the harborview any more than I would regard a sailboat—just a machine, after all, for harvesting the wind—as polluting it, or a surfer as sullying the wave he rides. There is aesthetic pleasure in ancient and appropriate ways of working with nature.

In these changing times it is necessary for our landscape painters, that traditional Cape type, to eliminate increasing portions of the actual scene. I spend a certain amount of time at galleries and have yet to see a painting of the Cape Cod Mall or Route 6 traffic. My guess is that in producing an aesthetically pleasing picture of our harbor painters are finding it convenient to ignore certain recently erected, overlarge houses pushing up from the dunes to maximize their view. I imagine these same painters are having no problem including the local shellfish industry doing its thing on the flats.

THE TABOO LOGIC
OF MUTUAL BACK-
SCRATCHING

BREWSTER'S BRIEF ERA of differential taxation for residents and non-residents raises the whole question of favoritism toward locals. The nonresident taxpayers who bitterly criticized the scheme counted heavily on a climate of opinion in which mutual back-scratching is seen even by potential beneficiaries as unfair.

One e-mail from a recently washed-ashore fulltime resident responding to my recent column on the nonresident power movement complained about differential pricing whether in taxing or pricing by businesses: "Fairness dictates that all Americans be treated equally." Sounds right. But what do we do with the tradition of local businesses giving a break to Americans who live here fulltime over those who drop in for a week or two in the good weather? In our town the two all-winter restaurants, as soon as the bulk of part-timers are gone, begin to run much-appreciated lunch specials as a way of acknowledging the reality of the local family budgets. Our local theater, when it broke the $20 a ticket barrier, gave a modest break to locals, perhaps as a way of saying: this is still, despite our having been noticed by big city newspapers, a local place with local sensibility.

Insofar as we are all, year-rounders and seasonal res-idents alike, just Americans or world citizens or neighbors, the Brewster nonresidents' favorite term (as in: This taxing favoritism is driving a wedge between neighbors), differential treatment would seem to be not only unfair but, like all prejudice, without rational basis. But if you think about it a bit there is, beyond the economic incentive of businesses, a logical basis for favoritism. Fulltime neighbors are in fact worth more than fairweather ones not in being intrinsically better people but simply by dint of being fulltime: more likely to be there when you need a favor, to help out on a project, simply to create a moment's warmth at the library or post office in the long, dreary winter, to provide the comfort of "we're all in this together."

Why shouldn't appreciation of deeper, time-tested relationships, trust of the sort only sharing a condition over time creates, find expression in business and town policy?

For a few years now there has been a controversy over a large house under construction on the dunes of Truro. The owners got a permit but were required not to disturb the dunes, which are considered a public resource. It is not an easy thing to build on dunes and yet not disturb their natural flow. Not surprisingly they ended up disregarding the condition, so the conservation board ordered a work stoppage until a dune-kindly (and expensive) solution could be worked out. These nonresident taxpayers from the Midwest have had a very rough time in being required to follow the law governing houses aspiring to a big view in Truro.

Some time into the above controversy I became aware of a house being built in another environmentally delicate waterfront situation here in Wellfleet in the Seashore Park. The owners, wanting to convert the tiny cottage with which they had made do for the 40 years into something resembling a real house had to contend with strict Seashore regs restricting rebuilds to the size of the original footprint. Impatient with the feet-dragging, as they saw it, of the park permitting process, they took a fast-track approach and started construction without official blessing, even though what they built seemed clearly a violation of the spirit and probably of the letter of the Seashore restrictions. They got away with it, eventually, I believe, wangling permission for the fait accompli. The Truro project last time I heard is in an indefinite stall.

Seems like a good example of favoritism to locals. Is it unfair? I don't think so. The Wellfleet waterfront house, while not strictly by the books, is in fact more appropriate to its setting than the Truro trophy house. That appropriateness, in turn, is not unrelated to the localness of the owners. As longtime member of the neighborhood and the larger community—several generations of this family have been part of the fabric of this town for decades—they naturally built with a sensibility attuned to the situation, the neighbors, and community standards. The modest house is in scale with other houses in the immediate vicinity. It has nothing of the trophy house about it. Local officials would have less motivation than those of Truro to hold them strictly to the letter. The Truro family, no doubt fine people but lacking history and knowledge and relationship with the neighbors and the community in general, built inappropriately by community standards, and have deserved to get no break.

Localness—trust, communal feeling, shared values, the sort of stuff that comes only by living many years in a place—is not just a sentimental, but a substantive factor. It is worth a great deal and even if the law can't always discriminate, it will and probably ought to find its way into the de facto handling of local affairs.

S. T. A. B. L. L.

I'M LOOKING FOR A CATCHY ACRONYM this morning, in connection with the interesting proposal that Wellfleet, already the self-styled gallery town and oyster capital of the world, become as well the garbage composting capital of the Lower Cape. I'm looking for an alternative to NIMBY as a way of understanding this issue.

Even though Big Garbage would seem to have an uphill battle in Wellfleet, those opposed to becoming the regional trash center—and that would seem to include about everybody except the enterprising selectman who came up with the idea and the company that wants the business— should not go down in history tarred with the NIMBY accusation.

On June 27 a meeting was held in the elementary school at which representatives of Waste Options Inc. were to explain their composting system to locals and answer questions. The feisty citizens present— approximately 100% opposed—were less interested in the details of the technology involved than in where it would be located. They wanted to know why the only town mentioned in the papers as a possible site for the big composter was Wellfleet. The company said that no site had been chosen; let us do our feasibility study, don't prejudge the idea. Feasibility smeasibility, said those present, we know enough already to know we don't want this. Where is it going to go?

Four months later we are still waiting for the other shoe to drop, the feasibility study. The real discussion of this, it is asserted in some quarters, cannot take place until we hear the company's proposal in detail. But it seems to me that what people at the June meeting were saying is that feasibility study starts with us. As those who will use it and have to live with it, we are key elements in the system and we are saying we won't play. End of feasibility study.

Those opposing Wellfleet as a trash center might be relieved if some other town were to step forward for the honor, but in fact no other town has stepped forward and no one's holding his or her breath (so far). Basically, when it comes to regional trash, it's not a NIMBY situation but NABY: Not in Anyone's Back Yard.

It isn't the composting technology that's at issue. It's the whole idea of regionalizing trash that's the Achilles heel of this proposal.

The composting idea seems to work well for Nantucket. If we were to use it here in Wellfleet in a scaled-down version, it would make an honest dump out of us again, instead of just a temporary resting place for stuff to be processed elsewhere. (Ever since we became a transfer station in the '80s we have been operating from a de facto NIMBY policy.) But the company says it will only work regionally—something about critical mass. It's one thing to take care of your own garbage and another to be everyone else's backyard, trash center for the entire region. In our town a wonderful rural section would become a sacrificial zone. But more damaging than whatever smell and endless rumbling of trucks will afflict the immediate area is the idea that will pollute the whole town: that we have become the repository of the region's trash.

Regionalization is a nice idea—eliminates redundancy, makes for greater efficiency, saves everyone money. But in some cases it doesn't work. Efficiency isn't everything. Certain things just don't regionalize well. Take nukes: if every place had to deal with its own nuclear waste I doubt we would ever have had a nuclear power industry. We may be relieved that Nevada, which most of the nation thinks of as being a desert inhabited only by one-armed bandits, has been volunteered for the job but does anyone think that's fair? Did the local opposition in that case deserve the NIMBY label?

According to a recent *New Yorker* piece, NIMBY has spawned two new acronyms, both of which would seem to be more appropriate for the nuclear waste situation: BANANA: Build Almost Nothing Anywhere Near Anyone. And NOPE: Not On Planet Earth.

Trash on the Outer Cape seems to be one of those things that works better if kept local. So far I've come up with LETKOG: Let Each Town Keep its Own Garbage. YOGDSAB: Your Own Garbage Doesn't Smell As Bad. Clear on the concept, but falling somewhat short in that all-important catchiness factor. MBIFBOFMOG (My Backyard is Fine, But Only For My Own Garbage)? I don't think so.

How about STABLL: Some Things Are Better Left Local. That might do it.

THANKS

FIRST OF ALL, I am grateful to Bill Breisky, editor of the *Cape Cod Times* at the time, for being so receptive back in 1994 to the suggestions of a relatively new resident. I first called him after a big nor'easter, about which I thought there had been too little ado made in the paper, to suggest that there ought to be a regular column on the weather in this area with such interesting weather. He said: Why don't you come down and talk? I did and somehow ended up with space in which to write about the weather and anything else I fancied about the local scene.

Thanks to Tony Kahn for welcoming me to the *Banner* a couple of years later.

Thanks to Tony and to Bill Smith, Tim White and Bill Mills, editorial page editors at the *Times* over the years, for the forbearance in leaving my stuff intact for the most part; and also for the occasional adroit intervention.

Thanks to all those readers who have over the years taken the time to write, e-mail or call to congratulate, commiserate or argue. Such response makes more of a difference than you might think. (And thanks to all the rest of you for simply being too speechless with admiration or profound emotion to manage a response.)

Thanks to my old friend and brother-in-law, Bob Pearson, for influencing me with his perspective on an early stage of this book.

On the home front, thanks to my son Ben for the insights into the life of this town I have been afforded by his growing up here—as well as for his help in the final stages of designing and formatting. And most especially, thanks to my wife Sue for putting up with my moods at various stages of the production of columns, and for loyally reading them all even though she had heard it all before.